Motor Vehicle
Basic Principles

By the same author

Fundamentals of Motor Vehicle
Technology (with F. W. Pittuck)

Motor Vehicle Technology;
Associated Studies 1 and 2

Auto Mate

Fundamentals of Automotive Electronics

Motor Vehicle Basic Principles

V.A.W. Hillier T.Eng.(CEI), FIMI, AMIRTE
Senior Lecturer in Automobile Engineering,
Croydon College

Stanley Thornes (Publishers) Ltd

Originally published in 1976 by Hutchinson Education
Reprinted 1977, 1979, 1982, 1983, 1985, 1986, 1987

Reprinted 1989 by
Stanley Thornes (Publishers) Ltd
Old Station Drive
Leckhampton
CHELTENHAM GL53 0DN

ISBN 0 7487 0276 8

Printed and bound in Great Britain at
The Bath Press, Avon.

Contents

Preface   7

1   Layout of Vehicle

1.1   Principal Components   9
1.2   Types of Chassis Layout   14
1.3   Review Questions   18

2   The Engine

2.1   Operating Principles of Engines   20
2.2   The Petrol–fuel System   31
2.3   Ignition System   38
2.4   Compression-ignition Engines   40
2.5   Engine Cooling   44
2.6   Engine Lubrication   48
2.7   Review Questions   50

3   The Transmission System

3.1   The Clutch   55
3.2   The Gearbox   57
3.3   Propeller Shafts and Universal Joints   62
3.4   Final Drive and Differential   65
3.5   Review Questions   70

4   Suspension and Body Construction

4.1   Springs and Dampers   73
4.2   Independent Suspension   77
4.3   Wheels and Tyres   78
4.4   Body Construction   82
4.5   Review Questions   85

5   Steering and Braking Systems

5.1   The Steering System   88
5.2   Braking System   90
5.3   Review Questions   95

6   Electrical System

6.1   Electrical Terms   97
6.2   Main Electrical Components   98
6.3   Review Questions   107

7   Appendix

7.1   Answers to Review Questions   109
7.2   English–American Glossary   110

Index   111

Preface

A modern motor vehicle is a complex piece of machinery which requires careful attention to make it perform in a safe, economical and efficient manner. To help the mechanic to achieve these ideals, vehicle manufacturers publish detailed service manuals, but the information presented generally assumes that the reader understands the basic principles underlying the construction and operation of the main vehicle components.

One purpose of this book is to present a simple explanation of the basic theory surrounding the various practical tasks which could be undertaken by a newcomer to this field of activity. Exposure to the technical terms and systems is intended to help the reader to acquire sufficient knowledge and confidence to understand the technical literature associated with routine maintenance of modern vehicles.

Long, lengthy descriptions of components have been avoided; instead the text has been restricted to a summary of the essential facts associated with each topic. Diagrams have been extensively used to indicate the basic construction and operation. It is anticipated that considerable time and mental energy will be saved by presenting the subject in a 'fact book' style. Many of the diagrams have been drawn in a detailed pictorial form; when the reader is following a course of technical studies, these diagrams will compliment the blackboard sketches presented by a lecturer.

The depth and range of subjects is similar to that required by the City and Guilds of London Institute for the Motor Vehicle Technology section of the examination: Motor Vehicle Craft Studies Part 1 (380). It is intended that the book will also form an introduction to the subject of Motor Vehicle Work for many other parties.

The inclusion of many multiple choice objective type questions at the end of each chapter should enable the reader to measure the progress along the road of technical competence.

V. A. W. Hillier 1976

1 Layout of Vehicle

1.1 Principal Components

Motor vehicles are made up from many separate items; these are fitted together to make units or *components* which in turn are mounted onto either a frame or body shell to form a *chassis*. The chassis comprises the following:

(a) Frame or body shell – forms the skeleton of the vehicle.

(b) Engine – acts as the power unit.

(c) Transmission – conveys the drive to the wheels.

(d) Suspension – absorbs the road shocks.

(e) Steering – controls the direction of movement.

(f) Brakes – slows down the vehicle.

(g) Electrical equipment – provides lighting, engine starting and other driver needs.

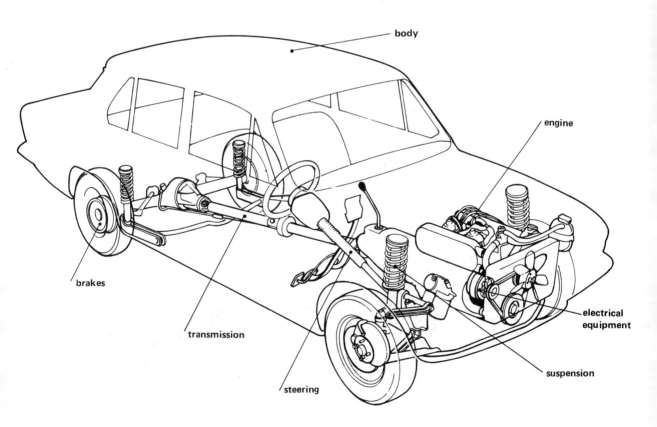

(a) *Frame or body shell*

Commercial vehicles normally use a separate steel frame to provide the rigidity needed to support the various loads. The two long *side members* of *channel* section are riveted to a number of *cross members* to give a low weight frame which offers great resistance to bending, twisting and lozenging.

Very few cars use separate frames, instead the body shell acts as the skeleton around which the vehicle is built. This *integral* type of body is made up from very thin, soft, steel sheet which is pressed into various shapes and welded together to form a very rigid, but lightweight unit.

(b) *Engine*

The *internal combustion* engine is most common: this obtains its power by burning a liquid fuel inside the engine cylinder. There are two types of engine:

1 spark-ignition,
2 diesel (also called a compression-ignition engine).

Damage will result if an engine is run on the incorrect fuel.

Both engines are called heat engines; the burning fuel generates heat which causes the gas inside the cylinder to increase its pressure and supply power to rotate a shaft connected to the transmission.

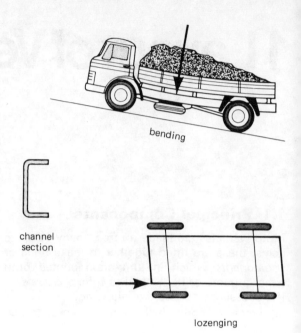

bending

channel section

lozenging

twisting (torsion)

Frame distortion

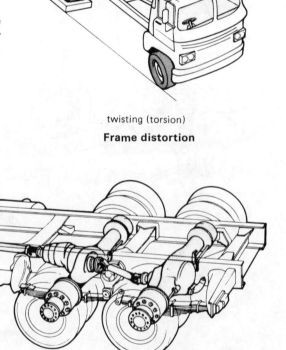

Layout of heavy commercial vehicle

Type	Uses	Fuel	Means of ignition
Spark-ignition	Cars	Petrol (gasolene)	Electric spark
Diesel (Compression-ignition)	Light and heavy commercial vehicles and taxis	Diesel oil (Derv)	No special ignition system necessary – fuel sprayed into the cylinder is fired when it contacts the very hot air

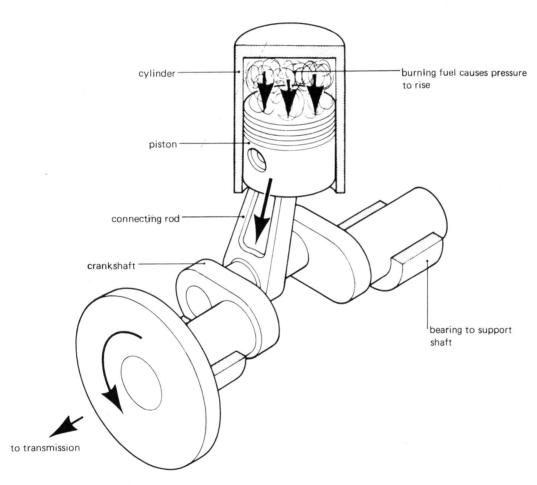

Gas pressure causes turning action

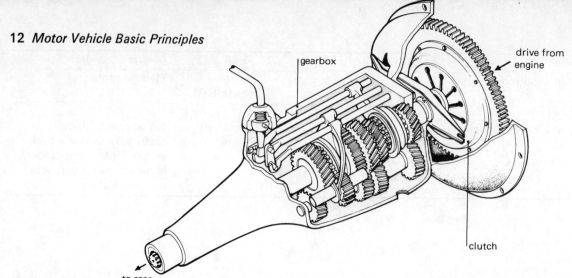

(c) *Transmission*

The transmission system applies to the components needed to transfer the drive from the engine to the road wheels. The main components and their purposes are:

1 clutch
  – to disengage the drive
  – to provide a smooth take-up of the drive

2 gearbox
  – to increase the turning effort (torque) applied to the driving road wheels
  – to enable the engine to operate within a given range of speed irrespective of the vehicle speed

3 final drive
  – to give reverse motion of the vehicle
  – to provide a neutral position so that the engine can run without moving the vehicle
  – to turn the drive through 90°
  – to reduce the speed of the drive by a set amount to match the engine to the vehicle

4 differential
  – to allow the inner driving road wheel to rotate slower than the outer wheel when the vehicle is cornering, whilst at the same time it ensures that a drive is applied equally to both wheels

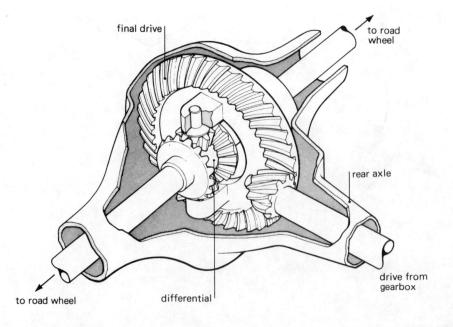

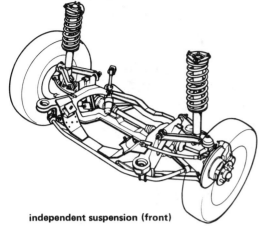

independent suspension (front)

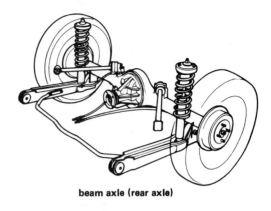

beam axle (rear axle)

(d) *Suspension*

The suspension covers the arrangement used to connect the wheels to the body. The purpose is to prevent large shocks, caused by the wheels striking bumps in the road, being passed to the vehicle occupants and components; otherwise discomfort and damage would occur.

The deflection of a pneumatic tyre takes much of the impact from a road bump but some form of springing is still needed to give a satisfactory ride. Unfortunately the release of the energy contained in a spring when it has been deflected by a road bump causes the vehicle to bounce, so to overcome this a damper (shock absorber) is fitted.

There are two suspension systems:

1 beam axle – the two wheels are mounted onto an axle which is connected to the chassis frame by strong springs,

2 independent suspension – each wheel is connected individually to the chassis frame by means of a linkage which incorporates a very flexible spring.

(e) *Steering*

This is achieved by turning the front wheels. The clearance required for this movement controls the layout of a car in respect to the seating arrangement. A large force is needed at the road wheel to steer or turn the vehicle onto a new course so a system of levers is provided between the steering wheel and the road wheel.

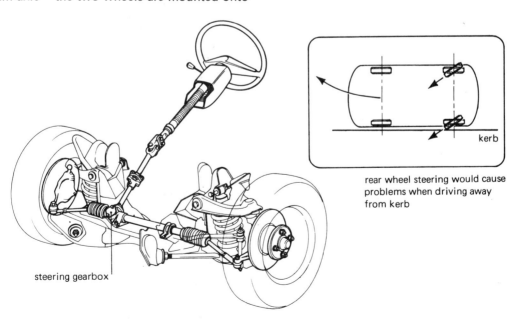

kerb

rear wheel steering would cause problems when driving away from kerb

steering gearbox

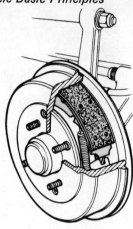

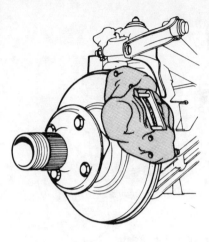

drum brake

disc brake

(f) *Brakes*

A brake is provided at each wheel to enable the driver to reduce the speed of the vehicle. This is achieved by converting the energy stored in the moving vehicle to another form of energy; heat. Expressed in a technical manner — the brakes convert kinetic energy to heat energy; the rate that the energy is converted controls the rate at which the vehicle slows down. To withstand the high temperatures the rubbing or friction materials are made from an asbestos compound.

The brake may be of the *drum* or *disc* type; most systems are hydraulically operated.

(g) *Electrical equipment*

Electrical power to operate the numerous components is supplied by a:

1 generator driven by the engine,
2 battery when the engine is stationary

1.2 Types of Chassis Layout

Private Cars

A buyer of a car considers one or more of the following points when choosing a product:

1 number of seats, comfort and interior finish
2 body shape, colour and general styling features
3 engine performance in relation to maximum power, acceleration and fuel economy
4 comfort of ride including noise
5 handling qualities
6 reliability and maintenance costs
7 safety in relation to general handling and special features included to protect the occupants in the event of a collision

Engine position	Driving wheels	Advantages
Front	Rear	1 Fairly even load applied to each wheel 2 Main components easily removed 3 Simple type of universal joint is used
Front (mounted across the vehicle)	Front	1 Lower floor gives good cornering and low car gives small air resistance 2 Short car 3 Flat floor, no propeller shaft tunnel or gearbox protrusions 4 Majority of weight at front gives good grip and good cornering
Rear	Rear	1 Large load on driving wheels gives good grip 2 Compact layout, short car 3 Simpler drive shaft layout than f.w.d. (front-wheel drive)

8 initial cost
9 name of manufacturer

The manufacturer is in business to sell cars so he must design his product to meet the buyer's general requirements. Various engine and drive systems are used; each one has advantages which are shown in the table.

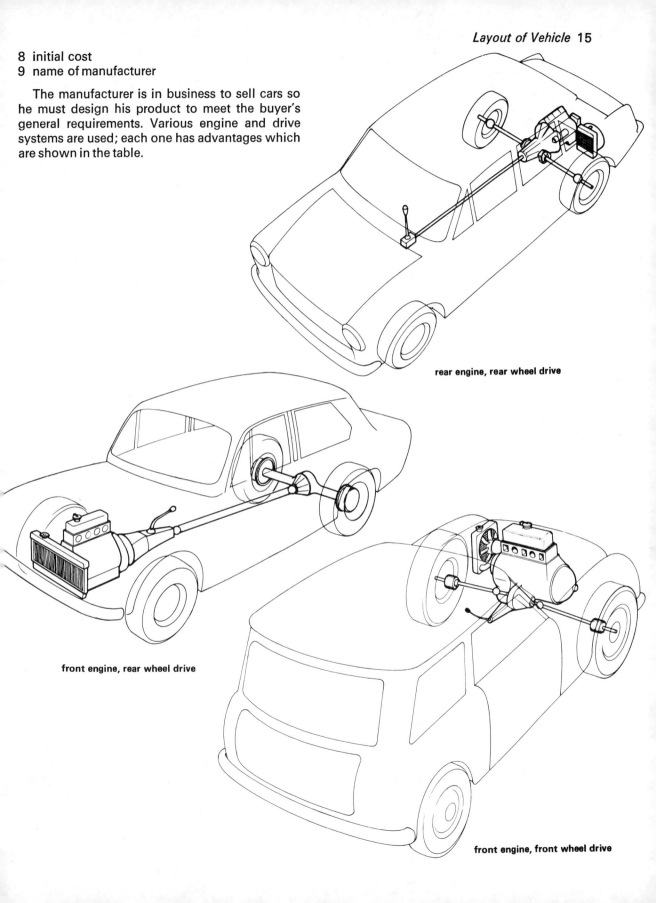

rear engine, rear wheel drive

front engine, rear wheel drive

front engine, front wheel drive

coupe

saloon

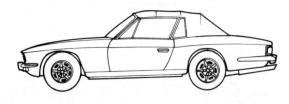

convertible

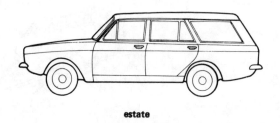

estate

Car body shapes are:

1 coupe (pronounced koo-pay) – originally a covered two seater
2 saloon – a covered car for four or more people
3 convertible (or drop-head) – a closed car which can be changed into an open car by removing or lowering the hood
4 estate (or shooting-brake or station-wagon) – a car with a roof extended to the rear to give more space for luggage

Vans

These are required by tradesmen to carry light loads over short distances; the size of the van is generally given as the maximum load which it is designed to carry. Many van components are interchangeable with those used on cars, but components such as clutches and suspension springs must be stronger to withstand the more strenuous duties.

Heavy Commercial Vehicles

These are very robust vehicles powered by a diesel engine and normally used for haulage work. The load carried generally requires twin tyres fitted side by side on the rear wheels and when the load is very heavy more axles are required. A heavy vehicle is defined as a vehicle which has a *gross vehicle weight* (g.v.w.) greater than about 3 tonne.

Rigid vehicles

These non-articulated vehicles are classified by the total number of wheels and the number of driving wheels, e.g. 6×4 indicates a six-wheeled vehicle having four driving wheels.

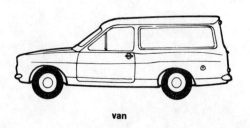

van

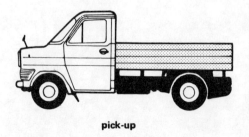

pick-up

4 x 2 rigid

6 x4 rigid (two driving axles)

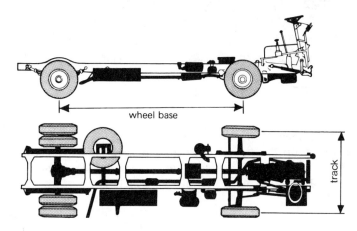

wheel base

track

4 x 2 rigid (forward control)

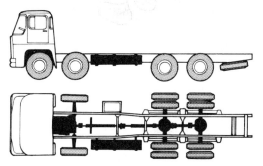

8 x 4 rigid (two driving axles, two steered axles)

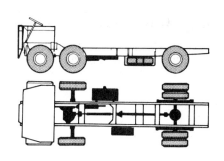

6 x 2 rigid

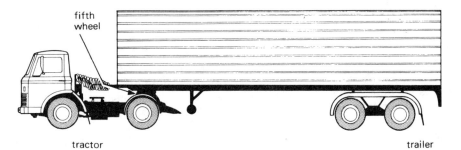

fifth
wheel

tractor

trailer

articulated vehicle

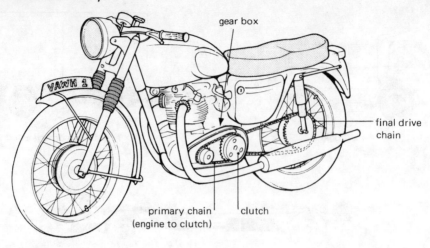

gear box

final drive chain

primary chain (engine to clutch)

clutch

Articulated vehicles

These consist of a detachable *trailer* which is supported on a platform on the *tractor* unit; the connection is called a fifth wheel. Loads carried must not exceed the gross train weight (g.t.w.)

Motor-cycles

Normally classified by the size of engine; the layout is shown above

1.3 Review Questions

1 When the main operating components are attached onto the main frame the assembly is called a
(a) unit
(b) chassis
(c) body shell
(d) sub-section

2 What term is used to cover the components which are fitted to form the drive line between the engine and road wheel?
(a) Transmission
(b) Suspension
(c) Final drive
(d) Power units

3 A frame consisting of side and cross members of channel section is normally used on
(a) light cars
(b) motor-cycles
(c) heavy motor cars
(d) heavy commercial vehicles

4 As the result of a collision one frame side member is set back in relation to the other side member. When the frame is set in this way it is said to be
(a) twisted
(b) torsioned
(c) lozenged
(d) extended

5 Most motor cars use a specially constructed body shell onto which is attached the main components. This construction is called
(a) channel
(b) integral
(c) separate
(d) independent

6 The type of engine used in most motor cars is
(a) internal combustion
(b) external combustion
(c) diesel
(d) compression-ignition

7 The type of engine used in heavy commercial vehicles is
(a) diesel
(b) petrol
(c) spark-ignition
(d) external combustion

8   The type of fuel and the means of ignition used with a motor car power unit are:

	Fuel	Ignition
(a)	derv	heated air
(b)	derv	electrical spark
(c)	petrol	electrical spark
(d)	petrol	heated air

9   Which transmission unit 'disengages the drive and provides a smooth take up of the drive'?
(a) Clutch
(b) Gearbox
(c) Final drive
(d) Differential

10   Which transmission unit 'allows the inner driving road wheel to rotate slower than the outer wheel but still maintains a drive to both wheels'?
(a) Clutch
(b) Gearbox
(c) Final drive
(d) Differential

11   The type of commercial vehicle which connects the tractor to the trailer by a fifth wheel coupling is called
(a) 6×5
(b) 8×5
(c) rigid
(d) articulated

12   Front-wheel steering is preferred to rear-wheel steering because the latter causes
(a) the differential to over-speed the wheels
(b) difficulties when moving away from the kerb
(c) the rear wheels to have a smaller turning circle
(d) difficulties because the front wheel speed is faster

13   The purpose of a suspension damper is to
(a) take the road shock
(b) prolong the bounce
(c) prevent the spring deflecting
(d) absorb the energy in the spring

14   The purpose of a brake is to
(a) lock the road wheel
(b) apply heat to generate kinetic energy
(c) convert kinetic energy to heat energy
(d) stop the drum or disc from rotating

15   Which one of the following car body shapes has the largest internal dimensions
(a) coupe
(b) saloon
(c) convertible
(d) estate

16   Which type of vehicle has the following advantage: even load applied to each wheel?

	Engine position	Driving wheels
(a)	Front	Rear
(b)	Rear	Front
(c)	Front	Front
(d)	Rear	Rear

17   As applied to the specification of a heavy commercial vehicle the abbreviation g.v.w. is
(a) general vehicle width
(b) gross vehicle weight
(c) gives variable wheelbase
(d) gross vehicle width

18   The distance between the centres of the front wheel is called the
(a) track
(b) wheelbase
(c) axle width
(d) turning circle

19   A commercial vehicle has two steered axles and two driving axles. This is called a
(a) 4×2
(b) 2×4
(c) 8×4
(d) 4×8

20   Normally the clutch is mounted between the
(a) engine and gearbox
(b) gearbox and propeller shaft
(c) propeller shaft and final drive
(d) final drive and differential

2 The Engine

2.1 Operating Principles of Engines

Gas Expansion

When a gas is heated it tries to expand — if this expansion is resisted then a high pressure is built up which in turn creates a large force.

A mixture of petrol and air compressed in a container, or cylinder, makes an explosive gas. When the gas is ignited the pressure moves the piston towards the open end of the cylinder.

Linking the piston by a connecting rod to a cranked shaft, causes the gas to rotate the shaft through half a turn. The power stroke 'uses up' the gas, so means must be provided to expel the burnt gas and recharge the cylinder with a fresh petrol–air mixture: this control of gas movement is the duty of the *valves;* an *inlet valve* allows the new mixture to enter at the right time and an *exhaust valve* lets out the burnt gas after the gas has done its job.

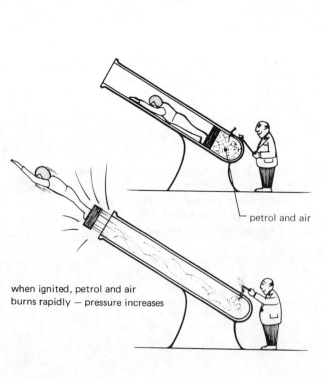

petrol and air

when ignited, petrol and air
burns rapidly — pressure increases

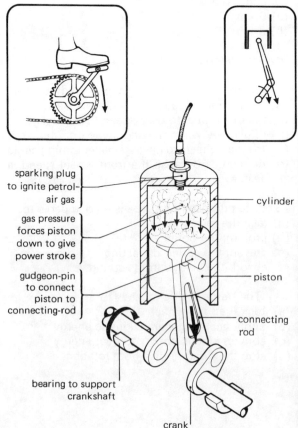

sparking plug
to ignite petrol-
air gas

cylinder

gas pressure
forces piston
down to give
power stroke

gudgeon-pin
to connect
piston to
connecting-rod

piston

connecting
rod

bearing to support
crankshaft

crank

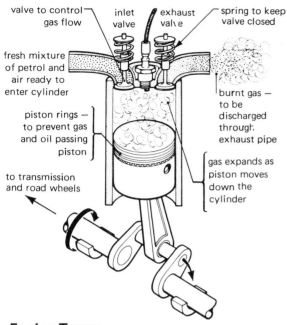

valve to control gas flow — inlet valve — exhaust valve — spring to keep valve closed

fresh mixture of petrol and air ready to enter cylinder

burnt gas — to be discharged through exhaust pipe

piston rings — to prevent gas and oil passing piston

to transmission and road wheels

gas expands as piston moves down the cylinder

engine capacity — this is the swept volume of all the cylinders e.g. a four-cylinder engine having a capacity of two litres (2000 cm^3) has a cylinder swept volume of 500 cm^3.

clearance volume — the volume of the space above the piston when it is at t.d.c.

$$\text{Compression ratio} = \frac{\text{swept vol} + \text{clearance vol}}{\text{clearance vol}}$$

Cycles of Operation

There are two ways in which an engine can be designed to operate:

1. two-stroke — a power stroke every revolution of the crank,
2. four-stroke — a power stroke every other revolution of the crank.

Four-stroke Spark-ignition Engine

Invented by Dr N. A. Otto it is often called the *Otto cycle* engine. The cycle of operations, or operating sequence, is spread over four piston strokes.

To complete the full cycle it takes *two revolutions of the crankshaft*.

The operating strokes are:

induction,

compression,

power,

exhaust.

Engine Terms

t.d.c. (top dead centre) — the position of the crank and piston when the piston is farther away from the crankshaft.

b.d.c. (bottom dead centre) — the position of the crank and piston when the piston is nearest to the crankshaft.

stroke — the distance between b.d.c. and t.d.c.; stroke is controlled by the crankshaft.

bore — the internal diameter of the cylinder.

swept volume — the volume between t.d.c. and b.d.c.

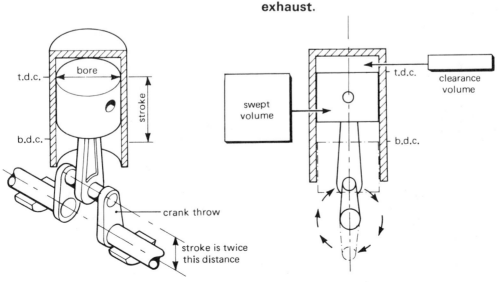

t.d.c. — bore — stroke — b.d.c. — crank throw — stroke is twice this distance

swept volume — t.d.c. — clearance volume — b.d.c.

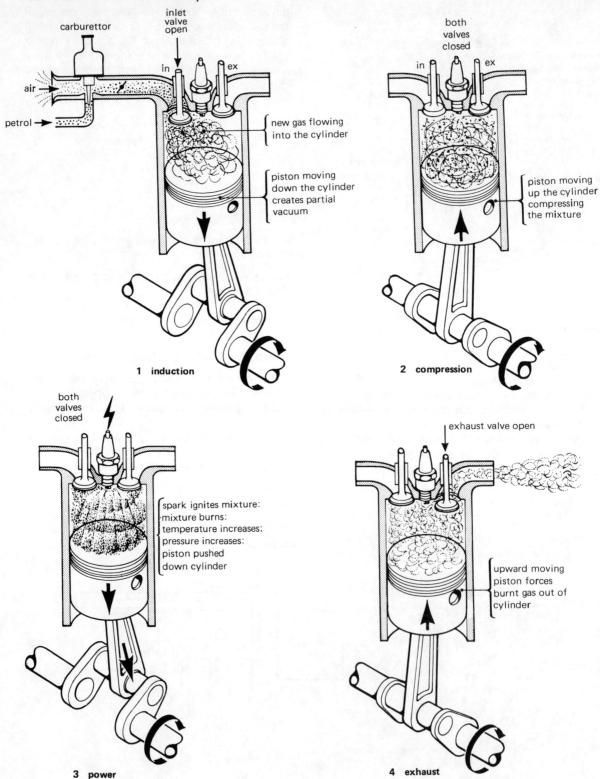

carburettor

inlet
valve
open

in   ex

air

petrol

new gas flowing
into the cylinder

piston moving
down the cylinder
creates partial
vacuum

1   induction

both
valves
closed

in   ex

piston moving
up the cylinder
compressing
the mixture

2   compression

both
valves
closed

spark ignites mixture:
mixture burns:
temperature increases:
pressure increases:
piston pushed
down cylinder

3   power

exhaust valve open

upward moving
piston forces
burnt gas out of
cylinder

4   exhaust

Four-stroke operation

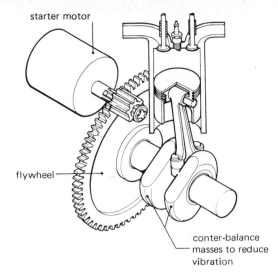

starter motor

flywheel

conter-balance masses to reduce vibration

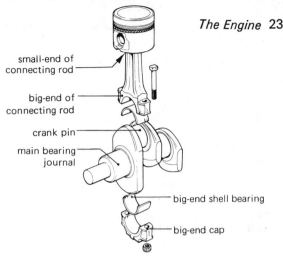

small-end of connecting rod

big-end of connecting rod

crank pin

main bearing journal

big-end shell bearing

big-end cap

Need for flywheel

There is only one working stroke in four so a flywheel is needed to drive the crankshaft during the time that the engine is performing the non-power strokes.

The flywheel 'carries' the engine over the non-working strokes.

Ignition timing

The compressed petrol–air mixture must be ignited at the correct instant so as to allow the maximum gas pressure to occur just after t.d.c. When the engine is idling (about 500 rev/min), ignition occurs when the piston is at:

top dead centre at the end of the compression stroke.

(The compression stroke can be found by noting the valve position or by the following:

1 remove sparking plug,
2 place thumb over plug hole and rotate engine.

(Air is pumped out during compression stroke.)

When the engine speed is increased the spark must occur earlier; this allows time for the mixture to burn.

To advance the spark means to make it occur earlier.
To retard the spark means to make it occur later.

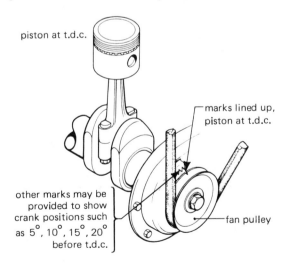

piston at t.d.c.

marks lined up, piston at t.d.c.

other marks may be provided to show crank positions such as 5°, 10°, 15°, 20° before t.d.c.

fan pulley

Location of T.D.C.

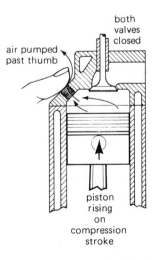

both valves closed

air pumped past thumb

piston rising on compression stroke

one method for finding the approximate position of 't.d.c. compression'

Valve Timing

Very old, slow speed engines had the following valve timing:

inlet valve – opens at t.d.c. and closes at b.d.c.
exhaust valve – opens at b.d.c. and closes at t.d.c.
   Modern engines operate at speeds as high as 6000 rev/min so to allow for this the valve timing is modified to:

inlet valve – opens just before t.d.c. and closes well past b.d.c.
exhaust valve – opens well before b.d.c. and closes just after t.d.c.

Valve Clearance

A clearance of about 0·3 mm (0·012 in) is given to ensure that the valve fully closes. The clearance is measured with a feeler gauge when the follower is on the back of the cam.

Valve timing for a modern engine

Valve Operation

A cam controls the opening and closing of a valve; the mechanism used depends on the position of the valves and camshaft.

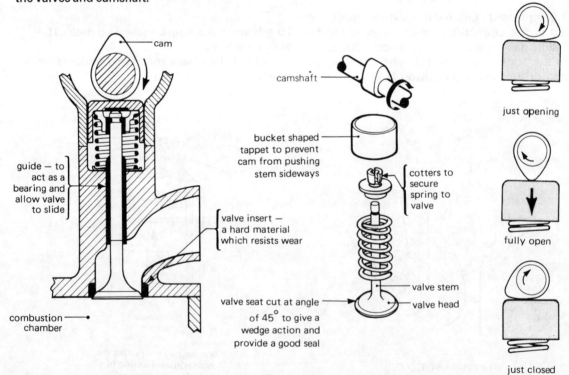

cam

camshaft

bucket shaped tappet to prevent cam from pushing stem sideways

guide – to act as a bearing and allow valve to slide

valve insert – a hard material which resists wear

combustion chamber

cotters to secure spring to valve

valve seat cut at angle of 45° to give a wedge action and provide a good seal

valve stem

valve head

just opening

fully open

just closed

Valve operation by overhead camshaft (O.H.C.)

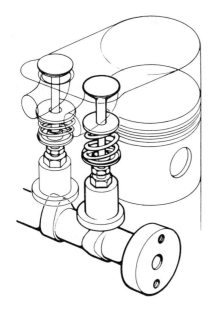

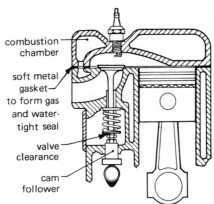

combustion chamber

soft metal gasket to form gas and water-tight seal

valve clearance

cam follower

**side valve engines are rarely used because: —
power output is low, fuel consumption is high**

Side valve engine

adjuster

rocker-arm

push-rod — to transmit motion from cam follower to rocker

cam follower

camshaft

inlet cam

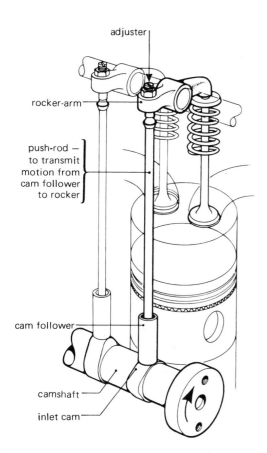

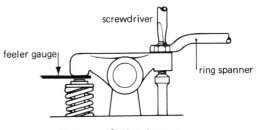

screwdriver

feeler gauge

ring spanner

adjustment of valve clearance

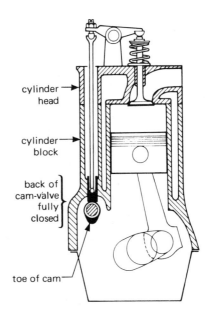

cylinder head

cylinder block

back of cam-valve fully closed

toe of cam

O.H.V. engine (overhead valve, side camshaft)

Each valve must operate once in every two revolutions of the crankshaft, so

camshaft rotates at half crankshaft speed.

The timing gears provide the reduction in speed. Marks on the gear help the mechanic to 'time the valves' (setting the camshaft to its correct position relative to the crankshaft).

Multi-cylinder Engines

A smoother flow of power from the crankshaft is obtained when more than one cylinder is used. The extra power inpulses are spaced out evenly throughout the two revolutions of the four-stroke cycle. The flywheel of a multi-cylinder engine is lighter in weight.

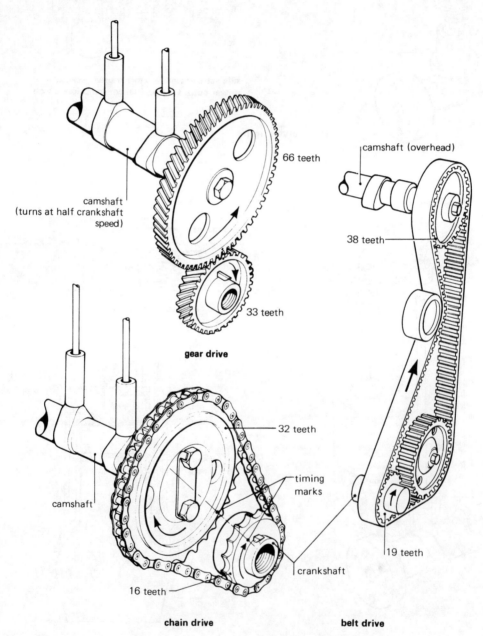

camshaft
(turns at half crankshaft speed)

66 teeth

33 teeth

gear drive

camshaft (overhead)

38 teeth

camshaft

32 teeth

timing marks

crankshaft

16 teeth

19 teeth

chain drive

belt drive

Camshaft drive arrangements

In-line Engines

The cylinders are placed in single row.

Twin cylinders

Used on motor-cycles and some small cars; one power stroke every 360° of crankshaft movement.

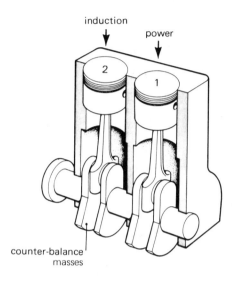

counter-balance masses

Crank position (degrees)	Cylinder no 1	Cylinder no. 2
0–180	Power	Induction
180–360	Exhaust	Compression
360–540	Induction	Power
540–720	Compression	Exhaust

Table 3

Four-cylinders

Commonly used on cars.

To give good balance the crankshaft is arranged such that when Nos. 1 and 4 pistons are at t.d.c., Nos. 2 and 3 pistons are at b.d.c.

Interval between power impulses is 180° (half revolution). The sequence diagram shows the events taking place in each cylinder. Firing order of this engine is 1342 but the order could be changed to 1243 if another camshaft was fitted. N.B. No. 4 piston is always performing the companion stroke to No. 1: when the inlet valve in No. 4 cylinder is fully open, No. 1 cylinder inlet valve is fully closed – this feature is useful to remember when checking valve clearances.

Check No. 1 valve when No. 8 is lifted.
Check No. 2 valve when No. 7 is lifted.
Check No. 3 valve when No. 6 is lifted.
Check No. 4 valve when No. 5 is lifted.
Check No. 5 valve when No. 4 is lifted.
Check No. 6 valve when No. 3 is lifted.
Check No. 7 valve when No. 2 is lifted.
Check No. 8 valve when No. 1 is lifted.

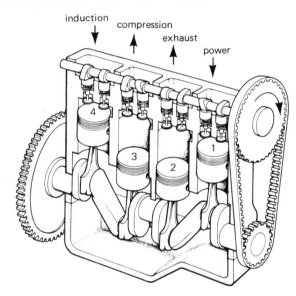

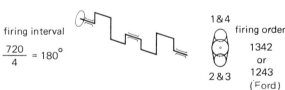

firing interval $\frac{720}{4} = 180°$

1 & 4
firing order
1342
or
1243
(Ford)

2 & 3

crankshaft throw arrangement

Crank position (degrees)	Cylinder no. 1	Cylinder no. 2	Cylinder no. 3	Cylinder no. 4
0–180	Power	Exhaust	Compression	Induction
180–360	Exhaust	Induction	Power	Compression
360–540	Induction	Compression	Exhaust	Power
540–720	Compression	Power	Induction	Exhaust

Six-cylinders

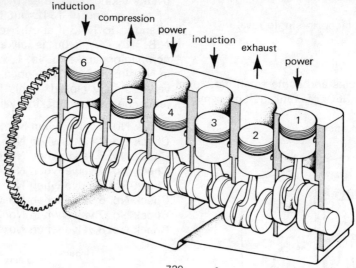

induction
compression
power
induction
exhaust
power

interval between power impulses $= \frac{720}{6} = 120°$ crankshaft movement

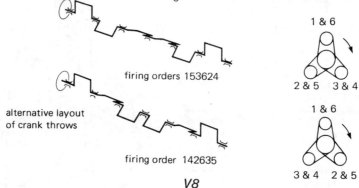

firing orders 153624

alternative layout of crank throws

firing order 142635

1 & 6

2 & 5   3 & 4

1 & 6

3 & 4   2 & 5

Vee Engines

Two rows of cylinders set in the form of a vee to give a compact arrangement.

V6

Two banks of three cylinders set at 60°.

V8

Two banks of four cylinders set at 90°.
British Standard Institute recommends that the right and left banks are called A and B respectively so:

firing order is A1, B1, A4, B4, B2, A3, B3, A2.

Many other firing orders are used.

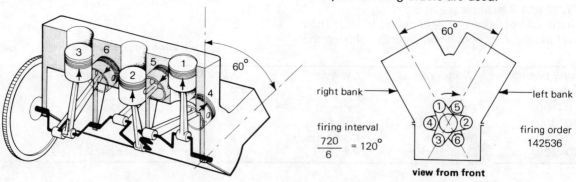

60°

firing interval

$\frac{720}{6} = 120°$

60°

right bank

left bank

firing order
142536

view from front

Six cylinders vee (V6)

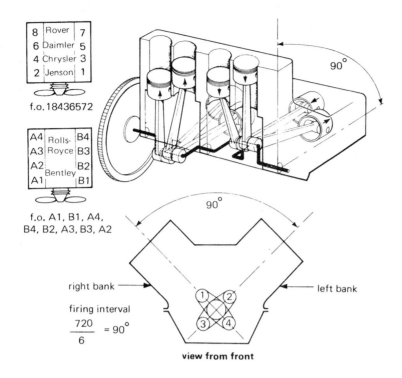

8	Rover	7
6	Daimler	5
4	Chrysler	3
2	Jenson	1

f.o. 18436572

A4	Rolls-	B4
A3	Royce	B3
A2	Bentley	B2
A1		B1

f.o. A1, B1, A4,
B4, B2, A3, B3, A2

right bank — — left bank

firing interval

$$\frac{720}{6} = 90°$$

view from front

Eight cylinders vee (V8)

Horizontally Opposed Engines

These engines are compact and due to the layout very little vibration is produced.

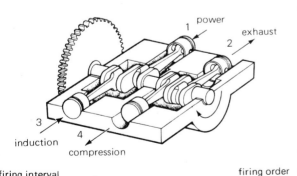

firing interval
$$\frac{720}{4} = 180°$$

firing order
1 4 3 2

Two-stroke Spark-ignition Engine

Two-stroke engines utilize both sides of the piston and use ports in the side of the cylinder to control the gas entering and leaving the cylinder.

The cycle of operations is completed in one revolution of the crank so a power stroke occurs every 360°.

Compared to a four-stroke engine the two-stroke unit has twice the number of power strokes per minute, but owing to inefficient charging of the cylinder the power output is less than double the power produced by the four-stroke.

Simple construction and smoothness in operation make the two-stroke suitable for small single-cylinder engines.

Lubrication of the working parts is provided by mixing a small quantity of oil with the petrol: a typical ratio of petrol to oil is 20:1.

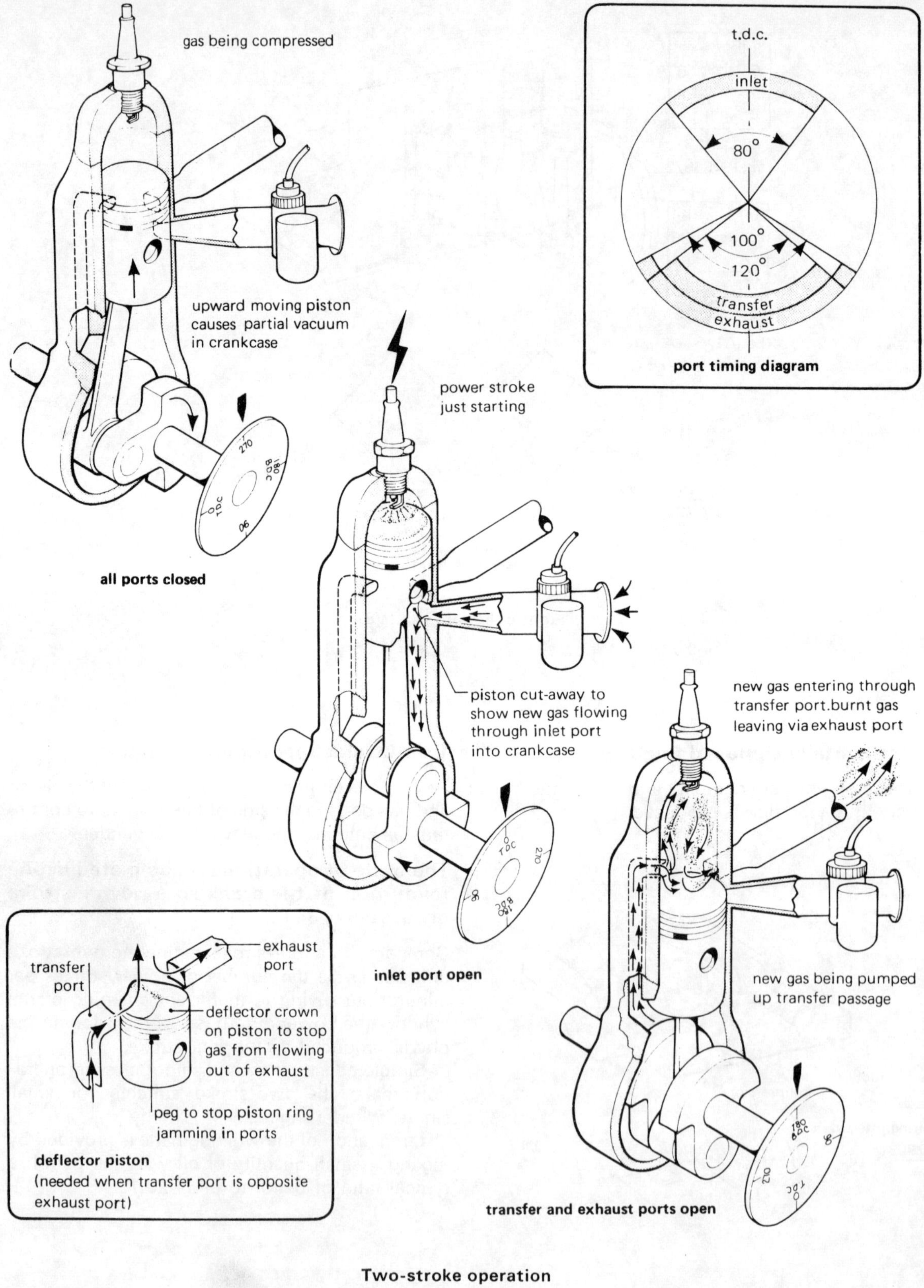
gas being compressed
upward moving piston causes partial vacuum in crankcase
270
180 BDC
TDC
90
all ports closed
t.d.c.
inlet
80°
100°
120°
transfer
exhaust
port timing diagram
power stroke just starting
piston cut-away to show new gas flowing through inlet port into crankcase
inlet port open
new gas entering through transfer port. burnt gas leaving via exhaust port
new gas being pumped up transfer passage
transfer and exhaust ports open
transfer port
exhaust port
deflector crown on piston to stop gas from flowing out of exhaust
peg to stop piston ring jamming in ports
deflector piston
(needed when transfer port is opposite exhaust port)

Two-stroke operation

2.2 The Petrol-fuel System

Air/Fuel Ratio

Petrol will not burn unless it is mixed with air: under ideal conditions the proportion of air to petrol required to burn the fuel completely is:

15 parts of air to 1 part petrol (by mass).

This means that 1 kg of petrol is mixed with 15 kg of air. The air/fuel ratio needed by a fuel to burn it completely is called the *chemically correct mixture*. The ratio 15:1 applies to petrol; other fuels have different ratios.

More air or less petrol, gives a *weak mixture;* i.e. an air/fuel ratio greater than 15:1 e.g. 20:1 is a weak mixture.

Less air or more petrol gives a *rich mixture*, i.e. an air/fuel ratio less than 15:1 e.g. 10:1 is a rich mixture.

Safety Precautions

1 **Petroleum spirit is highly flammable. A severe explosion can occur if a naked flame or electrical spark is brought into contact with petrol vapour which is trapped in a poorly ventilated work area.**
2 **Exhaust gas should be treated as poisonous. Do not inhale the exhaust gas from an engine.**

Mixture strength	Combustion	Exhaust gas	Effects
Very weak	Burns very slowly	Clean	High fuel consumption Low engine power Engine may overheat
Very rich	Burns slowly	Black or sooty and is poisonous – it contains carbon monoxide	Very high fuel consumption Low engine power

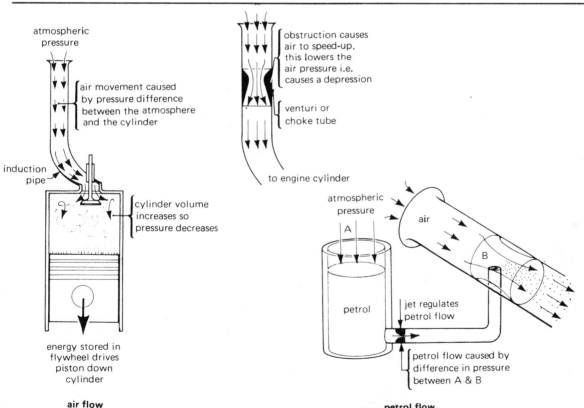

air flow

petrol flow

Principle of simple carburettor

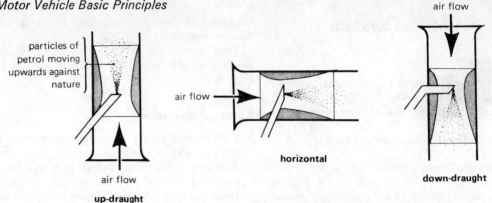

particles of petrol moving upwards against nature

air flow

horizontal

air flow

down-draught

air flow

up-draught
(rarely used today)

Direction of air-flow through carburettor

Engine Requirements

The fuel mixture supplied to an engine should be:

1 metered to give the correct air–fuel ratio,
2 broken up (atomized) into fine particles to make it burn quickly,
3 heated up (vaporized) to form a gas.

The carburettor performs tasks 1 and 2; the induction pipe joining the carburettor to the engine meets the other requirement.

Principle of a Simple Carburettor

The carburettor consists of two main points:

1 float chamber   — to regulate the flow of petrol to the carburettor
  — to maintain the petrol at a level just below the jet outlet

2 mixing chamber — to mix the fuel and air in the correct proportion
  — to atomize the fuel

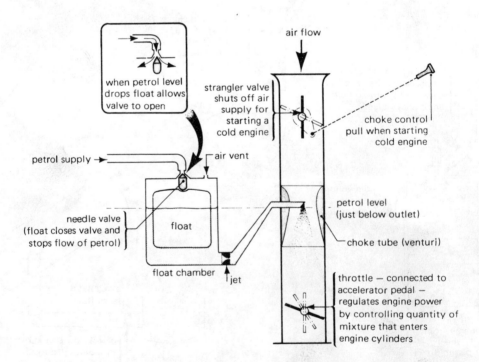

when petrol level drops float allows valve to open

strangler valve shuts off air supply for starting a cold engine

air flow

choke control
pull when starting cold engine

petrol supply →

air vent

needle valve
(float closes valve and stops flow of petrol)

float

petrol level
(just below outlet)

choke tube (venturi)

float chamber

jet

throttle — connected to accelerator pedal — regulates engine power by controlling quantity of mixture that enters engine cylinders

Layout of simple carburettor

Layout of a Simple Carburettor

Action of throttle

Opening the throttle valve causes the air flow through the carburettor to increase: this intensifies the depression in the choke tube and allows more fuel to flow from the float chamber to mix with this extra air. Unfortunately the petrol flow increases at a greater rate than the air supply so:

the mixture supplied by a simple carburettor gets richer as the speed is increased.

To overcome this problem a *correction* or *compensation system* is necessary.

Need for cold starting arrangement

A carburettor set to give a mixture strength of 15:1 at a normal engine speed would be unsuitable for starting a cold engine. This is because:

1 the cold engine will not vaporize the fuel,
2 the slow cranking speed only gives a small depression and this causes the carburettor to supply a very weak mixture.

3 petrol falls out of the slow moving air and is deposited in the walls of the induction pipe.

Shutting off the air supply by means of a strangler valve gives a rich mixture (about 8:1) and provides the engine with a sufficient number of fuel particles that vaporize easily.

Slow running

The small amount of air passing through the carburettor when the engine is slow running only produces a very small choke depression. This means that too little fuel will be supplied and the engine will stall.

The slow running system has an outlet in a region where a high depression exists when the engine is idling.

To obtain a smooth transfer as the engine speed is increased from idling, extra holes are drilled adjacent to the edge of the throttle disc: these holes are the *progression* outlets.

The adjusting screws control the slow running system; one screw sets the idling speed the other enables the slow running mixture to be varied to give the smoothest engine speed.

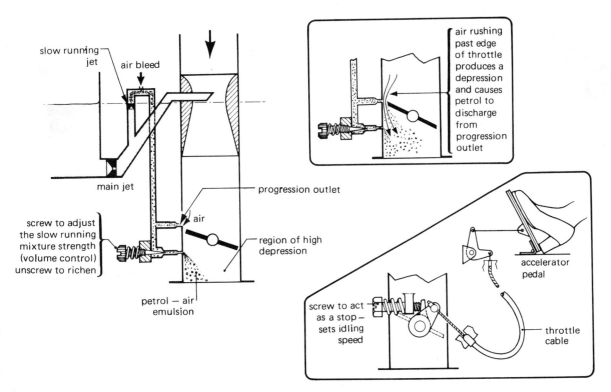

Slow running system

Carburettor Types

There are two basic types of carburettor:

1 constant choke – a fixed choke of a given diameter; the type already described,
2 constant vacuum or constant depression.

Constant vacuum carburettor

Has a variable choke which enlarges as the engine speed or load is increased. Opening the throttle causes the depression above the carburettor piston to increase; this causes the piston and tapered needle to rise a set amount and allows more petrol to mix with the larger quantity of air.

The air speed through the choke is constant over the whole speed range and this feature keeps the choke depression constant.

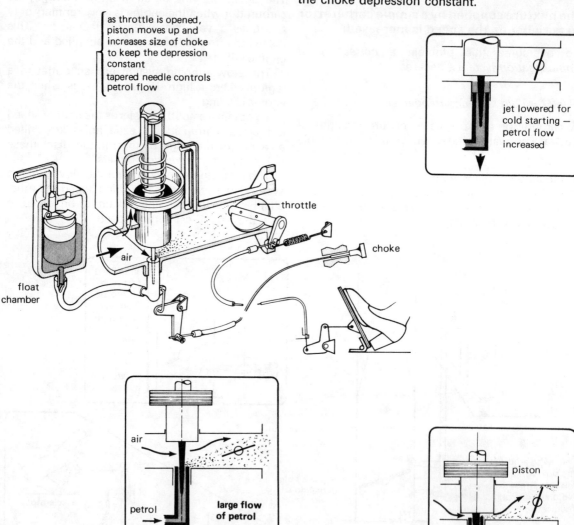

as throttle is opened, piston moves up and increases size of choke to keep the depression constant

tapered needle controls petrol flow

throttle

choke

air

float chamber

jet lowered for cold starting — petrol flow increased

air

petrol

large flow of petrol

jet
needle

plan view of needle and jet

piston

small flow of petrol

area of petrol exposed to air

Constant vacuum carburettor

Induction Manifold

When the engine has more than one cylinder the induction system is made in the form of a manifold. The arrangement used should:

1 distribute the air–fuel mixture equally,
2 enable the cylinders to receive a large quantity of mixture (give a good volumetric efficiency).

To meet these requirements more than one carburettor may be fitted.

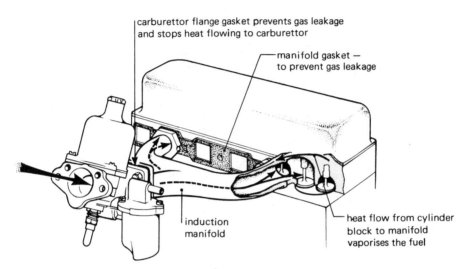

carburettor flange gasket prevents gas leakage and stops heat flowing to carburettor

manifold gasket — to prevent gas leakage

induction manifold

heat flow from cylinder block to manifold vaporises the fuel

four cylinder engine single carburettor

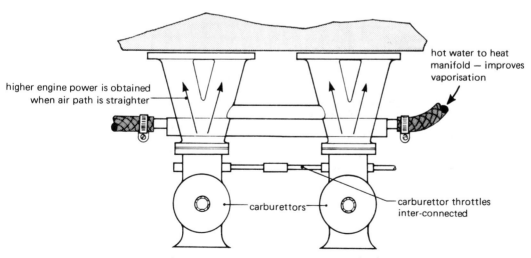

hot water to heat manifold — improves vaporisation

higher engine power is obtained when air path is straighter

carburettors

carburettor throttles inter-connected

four cylinder engine — twin carburettors (t.c.)

Induction manifolds

Air Cleaner

To reduce engine wear the air is filtered by passing it through a paper gauze which can be changed periodically.

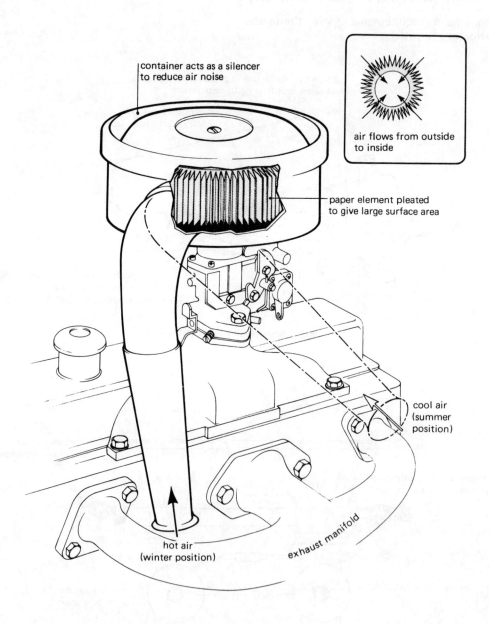

container acts as a silencer to reduce air noise

air flows from outside to inside

paper element pleated to give large surface area

cool air (summer position)

hot air (winter position)

exhaust manifold

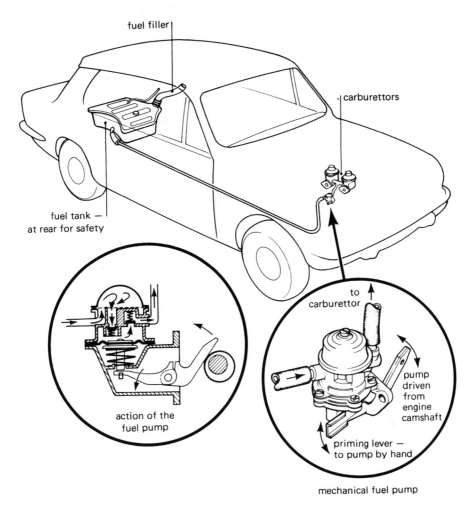

Fuel system – mechanical pump

Fuel System

Petrol is fed from the tank to the carburettor by a *fuel pump*. The pump may be:

1 electric – positioned close to the tank to avoid vapour-lock problems,
2 mechanical – positioned on the side of the engine and driven by the engine camshaft.

2.3 Ignition System

To start the petrol–air mixture burning, the sparking plug must give a good electrical spark; this must occur just before t.d.c. as the piston nears the end of the compression stroke.

Sparking Plug

Electrical energy supplied to the plug terminal is passed down the centre electrode and jumps across the air-gap to the earth electrode. Insulation around the centre electrode should prevent the electrical energy taking an alternative path to that required.

The voltage (electrical pressure) required to cause a spark at the plug gap depends on the:

1 gap between electrodes,
2 gas pressure in the cylinder.

It only requires about 600V to jump the plug gap at atmospheric pressure, whereas 8000V may be needed to produce a spark under cylinder operating conditions.

Production of a High-voltage Current

The twelve volts supplied by a battery is far below that required by a sparking plug, so a special system must be fitted.

Systems in use are:

1 coil ignition – majority of cars use this system;
2 transistorized – a modern system which is often required on eight-cylinder engines;
3 magneto – used on motor-cycles, this system is a self contained ignition unit that does not require a battery.

Coil Ignition

The main parts are:

Ignition coil

This transforms the battery voltage from 12V to that required to produce a spark at the plug.

Contact-breaker

A mechanically operated switch which breaks a low voltage circuit and causes the coil to produce a high voltage current. The timing of the spark is controlled by the contact-breaker. The cam

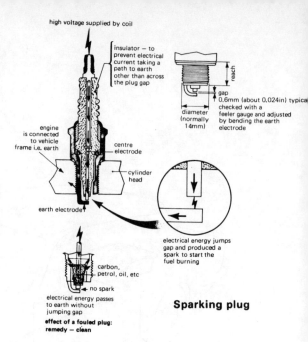

high voltage supplied by coil

insulator – to prevent electrical current taking a path to earth other than across the plug gap

reach

gap 0.6mm (about 0.024in) typical checked with a feeler gauge and adjusted by bending the earth electrode

diameter (normally 14mm)

engine is connected to vehicle frame i.e. earth

centre electrode

cylinder head

earth electrode

electrical energy jumps gap and produced a spark to start the fuel burning

carbon, petrol, oil, etc

no spark

electrical energy passes to earth without jumping gap

effect of a fouled plug: remedy – clean

Sparking plug

operating a four-stroke engine contact-breaker revolves at half crankshaft speed.

Distributor

Fitted to multi-cylinder engines this unit distributes the high-voltage current to the appropriate sparking plug.

Operation

When the ignition is switched 'on', current will flow through the low tension (primary) circuit. When the cam *opens* the contact-breaker, the low tension circuit is broken which causes the coil to produce a high voltage current: this is fed via the distributor to the sparking plug.

Excessive arcing at the contact-breaker and a quicker break of the circuit is made possible by fitting a capacitor (condenser). This unit acts as a 'buffer' to absorb momentarily the current during the time that the contacts are opening.

Automatic advance

A mechanism is incorporated in the distributor assembly (which also includes the contact-breaker unit) to vary the timing of the spark to suit the engine speed and load. A centrifugal device fitted under the contact-breaker base plate looks after the speed aspect; a vacuum arrangement adjusts for the load on the engine.

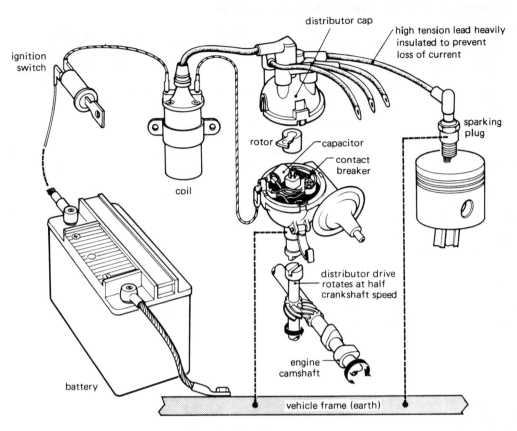

pictorial view of coil-ignition system

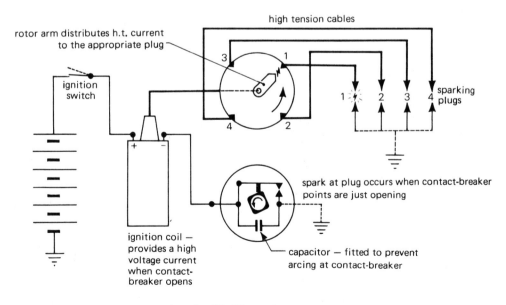

operation of coil-ignition system

2.4 Compression-ignition Engines (C.I. Engines)

This engine is commonly called a *diesel* engine. It gets this name from the pioneer work done by Dr Rudolf Diesel.

The diesel is used for the majority of heavy vehicles and the excellent fuel economy makes it an attractive alternative to the petrol engine for light commercial vehicles, delivery vans and taxis. Most of these vehicles use a four-stroke engine but two-stroke operation is favoured by a number of heavy vehicle operators.

Differences Between Diesel and Petrol

Compared to the petrol engine, the C.I. engine is different in the following ways:

Induction

Air only is supplied during the induction stroke and a full unthrottled charge is induced.

Compression

The air is more highly compressed; whereas a typical compression ratio of a petrol engine is 9:1, the ratio for a C.I. engine is about 16:1. This high compression results in the air being very hot at the end of the compression stroke.

Fuel supply

The fuel is a special gas oil called derv (diesel engine road vehicle). It is pumped at very high pressure into the cylinder when the piston is nearing the end of the compression stroke. Power output is controlled by regulating the quantity of fuel injected.

Ignition

No electrical spark is necessary since the high temperature of the air in the cylinder is sufficient to fire the fuel oil as it is injected.

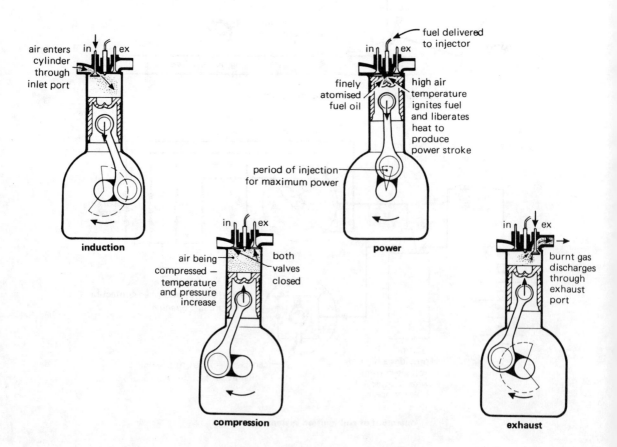

Four-stroke compression-ignition engine

Engine construction

High cylinder pressure demand a more robust engine construction. A governor is fitted to limit the engine speed to a safe figure.

Four-stroke C.I. Operating Cycle

Spread over two crankshaft revolutions or 720° the four strokes are:

induction, compression, power, exhaust.

Valve operation and timing is similar to the petrol engine.

Two-stroke C.I. Operating Cycle

This operating cycle has a power stroke every revolution; the cycle completed in one crankshaft revolution or 360°.

Two-stroke operation on the C.I. principle overcomes one of the main disadvantages of the two-stroke petrol engine; the loss of fuel when the transfer and exhaust ports are open at the same time. The new charge in a C.I. engine is air so no loss of fuel occurs at this stage; instead the air flow to the exhaust helps to clear the burnt gas from the cylinder.

Most of the two-stroke engines used on vehicles have a blower to pump the air into the cylinder.

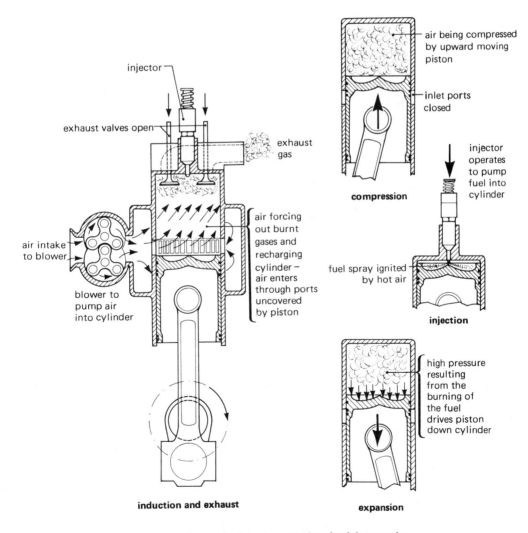

Two-stroke compression-ignition engine

Fuel-Injection System

The engine demands that the fuel supplied is:

1 timed to inject when the piston is near the end of the compression stroke,
2 atomized (broken-up) into fine particles;
3 forced with sufficient pressure into the hot, dense, turbulent air.

If these demands are not met, the engine will knock excessively and the exhaust will be dirty.

Since the power output of a cylinder is controlled by the quantity of fuel injected, the system must be calibrated to ensure that each one of the cylinders receives an equal amount of fuel: unbalance in this respect will cause a variation in the cylinder power output and result in rough running.

Fuel injection equipment is made to very close limits so:

to prevent wear great attention to filtration is necessary.

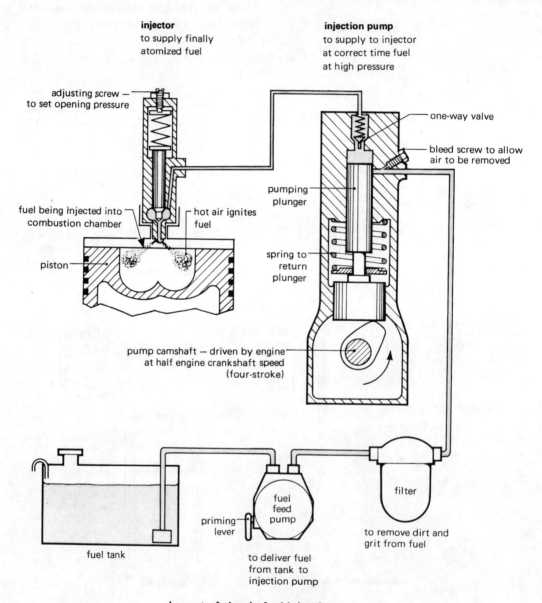

Layout of simple fuel injection system

Safety

Care must be exercised when working on the C.I. engine. The special safety precautions are:

1 **use a barrier cream on the hands to protect against the risk of dermatitis,**
2 **don't allow the spray from an injector to contact the skin. The high pressure can cause the fuel to penetrate human skin.**

Layout of system

Most engines use a jerk pump which builds up the pressure at the instant that injection is required.

The two common types of injection pump used are:

1 in-line – a series of separate pumping elements arranged side-by-side,
2 distributor (D.P.A.) – two opposed plungers supply the fuel under pressure to a rotor which distributes the fuel to the appropriate cylinder.

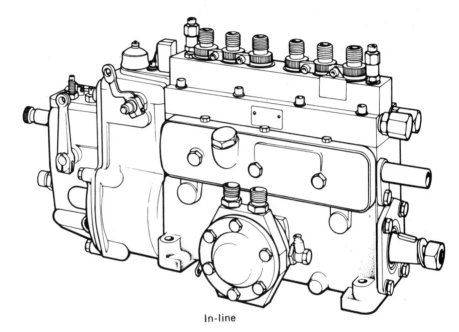

In-line

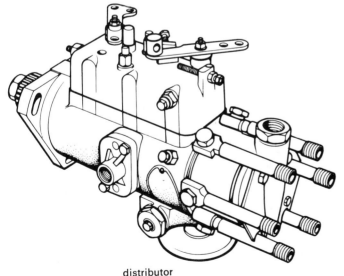

distributor

Types of injection pump

2.5 Engine Cooling

Some form of cooling must be provided to take away the heat from the cylinder and working parts of an engine. This heat comes from combustion of the fuel and from friction between rubbing parts.

An uncooled engine would result in:

1 seizure of working parts due to heat expansion,
2 excessive wear – the oil would be burnt,
3 pre-ignition of the petrol–air mixture. This means that the mixture would be ignited before time by some red-hot particle in the combustion chamber.

There are two methods of cooling:

1 air,
2 liquid.

Air Cooling

Most motor-cycle engines are air cooled. The principle is to fin the cylinder so as to increase the area of the hot surface exposed to the flow of cool air. This method of cooling is cheap, lightweight and is not subject to troubles such as leakage and freezing problems.

Airflow for cooling a multi-cylinder engine is provided by a centrifugal fan; this forces the air through ducted passages and over the finned cylinders.

Liquid Cooling

The majority of engines are water cooled because of the following advantages:

1 mechanical noise is reduced,
2 temperature of the various engine parts is more uniform.

In the past liquid cooling was achieved by *thermo-syphon* circulation: this relied on the natural change in density which occurred when the temperature of the water was varied.

The method of heat transfer is:

conduction, convection and radiation.

Conduction

The cylinder passes heat to the water in the jacket.

Convection

As the water is heated it gets lighter and rises to the heater tank in the radiator: cooler water from the radiator flows through the bottom hose to the water jacket.

Radiation

Hot water moving down through the radiator tubes gives up its heat to the air stream by radiation.

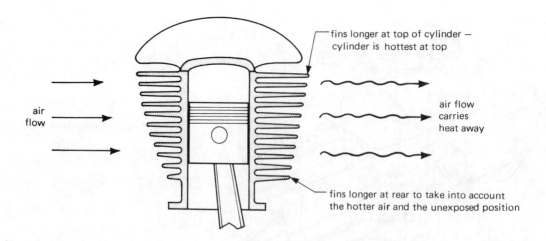

fins longer at top of cylinder – cylinder is hottest at top

air flow

air flow carries heat away

fins longer at rear to take into account the hotter air and the unexposed position

Air cooling

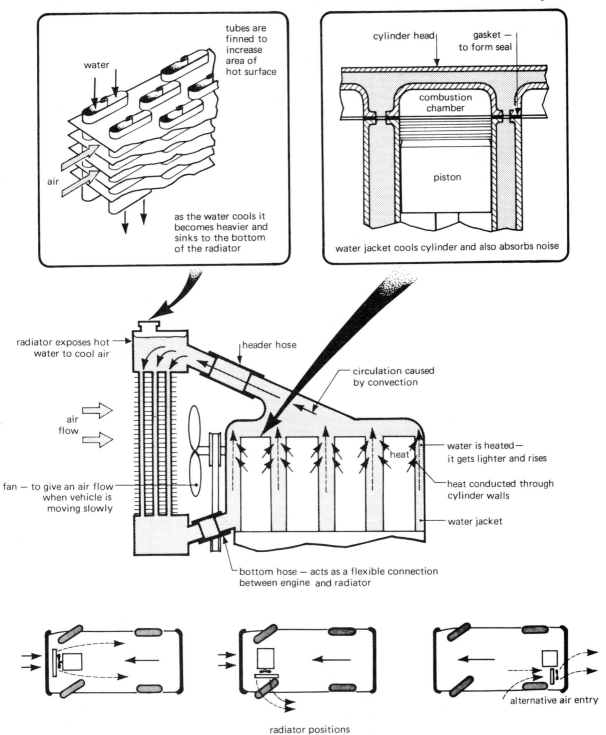

tubes are finned to increase area of hot surface

water

air

as the water cools it becomes heavier and sinks to the bottom of the radiator

cylinder head

gasket — to form seal

combustion chamber

piston

water jacket cools cylinder and also absorbs noise

radiator exposes hot water to cool air

header hose

circulation caused by convection

air flow

water is heated — it gets lighter and rises

heat

fan — to give an air flow when vehicle is moving slowly

heat conducted through cylinder walls

water jacket

bottom hose — acts as a flexible connection between engine and radiator

radiator positions

alternative air entry

Thermo-syphon cooling system

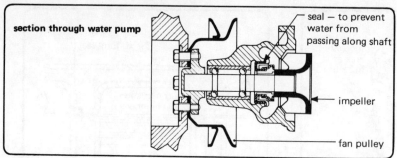

section through water pump

seal — to prevent water from passing along shaft

impeller

fan pulley

Pump assisted cooling system

Pump-assisted circulation

Natural thermo-syphon circulation had the disadvantages:

1 too slow in operation,
2 required a large quantity of water,
3 demanded a large, high radiator with a vertical flow.

To overcome these problems, modern engines use a pump-assisted system.

Thermostat

This is a heat sensitive valve which controls the water temperature by altering the speed of circulation. It is generally fitted on the engine side of the top hose and is pre-set to stop the water flow to the radiator when the coolant temperature is less than about 80°C.

The purpose of the thermostat is to:

1 allow the engine to warm up quickly. Engine wear, fuel consumption and power output are poor when the engine is operated at a low temperature.
2 prevent overcooling when the engine is running under a light load.

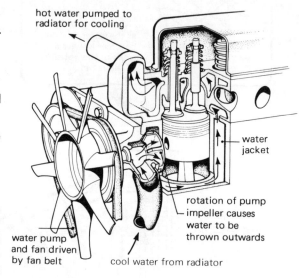

hot water pumped to radiator for cooling

water jacket

rotation of pump impeller causes water to be thrown outwards

water pump and fan driven by fan belt

cool water from radiator

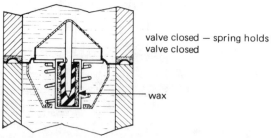

valve closed — spring holds valve closed

wax

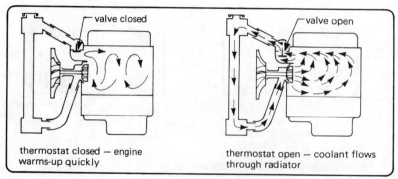

valve closed

valve open

thermostat closed — engine warms-up quickly

thermostat open — coolant flows through radiator

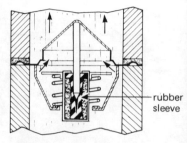

valve open — expansion of wax compresses rubber sleeve and pushes valve open

rubber sleeve

Thermostat operation (wax-element type)

Most modern engines use a thermostat of the *wax* element type; an older design called the *bellows* type is not suitable for present-day pressurized cooling systems.

Pressurized water cooling

Water subjected to atmospheric pressure boils at about 100°C. When the cooling system is pressurized, the increase in the boiling point enables the engine to operate at a higher temperature with the result that power, economy and engine life are all improved.

The operating pressure of the system is controlled by the radiator cap: the pre-set pressure of the cap is marked on the top surface.

Safety precautions when removing radiator caps. If the engine is hot:

1 **protect the hand with a heat-resistant glove,**
2 **remove the cap slowly to allow the pressure to release before the cap is detached,**
3 **the water may boil when the cap is removed.**

Anti-freeze

This is a solution which is added to the cooling system to lower the temperature at which freezing of the coolant occurs: the actual freezing temperature is governed by the quantity of anti-freeze added to the system.

Ice increases its volume as its temperature decreases, so extensive damage to the cylinder block will result if the coolant freezes.

Most modern anti-freeze solutions contain special chemical additives called inhibitors to reduce corrosion of the metal parts.

Care must be taken to avoid splashing anti-freeze on the vehicle paintwork, since some of the chemicals can soften the paint.

Anti-freeze is poisonous – it should not be kept in drink bottles.

Density of anti-freeze is different to water so it is possible to measure the strength of the anti-freeze mixture in a cooling system by using a special *hydrometer*.

Cooling system maintenance

The normal unsealed coolant system should have the coolant level checked and topped up (with pure water if possible) at weekly intervals.

Regular inspections should be made for:

1 leakage of the coolant, especially after filling with anti-freeze,
2 cracking or hardening of the flexible hoses,
3 tightness of the fan belt,
4 operating pressure of the radiator cap,
5 correct functioning of the thermostat.

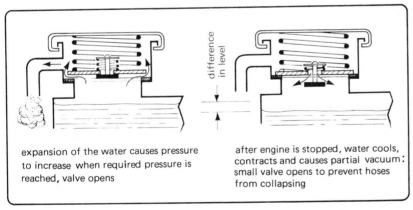

expansion of the water causes pressure to increase when required pressure is reached, valve opens

after engine is stopped, water cools, contracts and causes partial vacuum: small valve opens to prevent hoses from collapsing

Pressure radiator cap

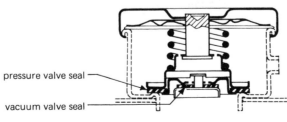

pressure valve seal

vacuum valve seal

2.6 Engine Lubrication

The friction between two surfaces rubbing together is reduced by using a lubricant to separate the materials. A flow of oil used for this purpose can also be used to carry away the excess heat from the metal parts.

Normally the engine manufacturer recommends a *mineral* oil of a given viscosity (thickness).

Oil is classified by the SAE number – the higher the number the thicker is the oil, e.g. an SAE 40 oil is thicker than SAE 20.

Lubricating System

The majority of engines use a *wet sump* system in which the engine sump acts as the reservoir.

Friction between engine components is reduced by:

1 boundary lubrication – relies on oil being *splashed* up onto the surfaces,
2 full film lubrication – an oil film is maintained by forcing the oil between the surfaces by an oil pump.

The system used on a modern engine combines both methods; pistons are lubricated by splash and bearings are pressure fed.

The main parts of a lubrication system are:

Pump

Driven by the camshaft, the pump forces the oil from the sump to the main oil gallery.

Main oil gallery

This runs the length of the engine. Drillings from the gallery allow oil to be supplied to the bearing surfaces.

Relief valve

Generally fitted in the gallery, this spring loaded valve opens when the pressure reaches the maximum allowed.

Filters

Beside the gauze screen that prevents pieces of metal entering the pump there is an external filter which can be renewed periodically.

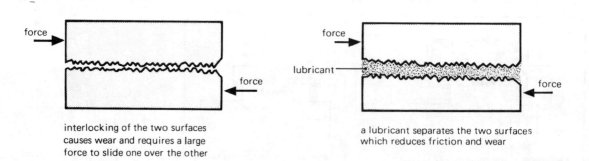

interlocking of the two surfaces causes wear and requires a large force to slide one over the other

a lubricant separates the two surfaces which reduces friction and wear

Action of a lubricant

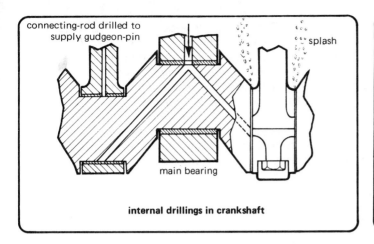

connecting-rod drilled to supply gudgeon-pin

splash

main bearing

internal drillings in crankshaft

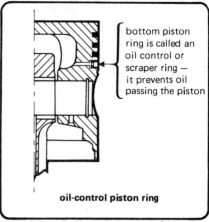

bottom piston ring is called an oil control or scraper ring — it prevents oil passing the piston

oil-control piston ring

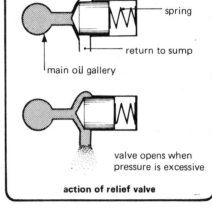

spring

return to sump

main oil gallery

valve opens when pressure is excessive

action of relief valve

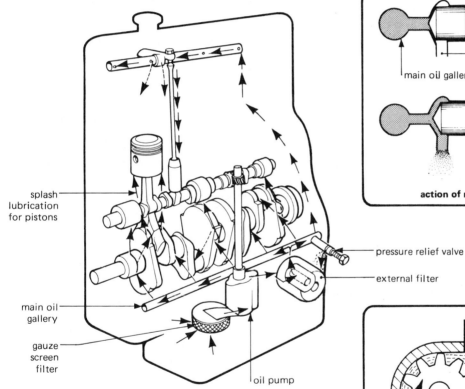

splash lubrication for pistons

main oil gallery

gauze screen filter

oil pump

pressure relief valve

external filter

Engine lubrication

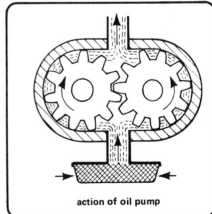

action of oil pump

2.7 Review Questions

1   The 'stroke' of an engine is the
(a) volume of the cylinder
(b) length of the connecting rod
(c) internal diameter of the cylinder
(d) distance between t.d.c. and b.d.c.

2   The purpose of a gudgeon pin is to
(a) prevent the valve from rotating
(b) link the connecting rod to the crankshaft
(c) secure the piston ring to the piston
(d) connect the piston to the connecting rod

3   How is the inlet valve opened and closed? It is opened by
(a) a cam and closed by a spring
(b) a spring and closed by a cam
(c) gas pressure and closed by a cam
(d) cylinder vacuum and closed by a spring

4   A four-cylinder engine has a capacity of 2·4 litres. The swept volume of one cylinder is
(a) 400 cm^3
(b) 600 cm^3
(c) 1200 cm^3
(d) 2400 cm^3

5   An engine has a clearance volume of 100 cm^3 and a swept volume of 800 cm^3. The compression ratio is
(a)   7:1
(b)   8:1
(c)   9:1
(d) 10:1

6   A single cylinder engine which has a power stroke every other revolution of the crank operates on a cycle called
(a) single-stroke
(b) two-stroke
(c) three-stroke
(d) four-stroke

7   After turning the crank of a single cylinder four-stroke engine through one revolution from the point where the spark occurs, the position of the valves will be

	Inlet	Exhaust
(a)	open fully	closed
(b)	closed	open fully
(c)	just closing	just opening
(d)	just opening	just closing

8   The operating sequence of an Otto cycle engine is; induction
(a) power, compression, exhaust
(b) exhaust, compression, power
(c) compression, power, exhaust
(d) power, exhaust, compression

9   A single cylinder, four-stroke engine is rotating at 2000 rev/min. The number of power strokes occurring in one minute is
(a) 500
(b) 1000
(c) 2000
(d) 4000

10   The stroke is increased when the
(a) piston is shortened
(b) connecting rod is lengthened
(c) crankshaft throw is lengthened
(d) gudgeon-pin is moved nearer to the crank-shaft

11   Ignition in an engine cylinder should occur at
(a) t.d.c. at the start of the compression stroke
(b) t.d.c. at the end of the compression stroke
(c) b.d.c. at the start of the power stroke
(d) b.d.c. at the end of the induction stroke

12   The engine component which 'carries' the engine over its non-working strokes is the
(a) piston
(b) flywheel
(c) crankshaft
(d) connecting rod

13   The purpose of valve clearance is to
(a) allow the valve to expand
(b) allow the valve to slide in the guide
(c) ensure that the valve closes fully
(d) ensure that the camshaft is free to rotate

14   To ensure combustion occurs at the correct time when the engine speed is increased, the spark should be
(a) advanced
(b) retarded
(c) less intense
(d) more intense

15   On modern four-stroke engines the exhaust valve opens just
(a) before t.d.c. and closes just before b.d.c.
(b) after t.d.c. and closes just before b.d.c.
(c) before b.d.c. and closes just after t.d.c.
(d) after b.d.c. and closes just before t.d.c.

16   On modern four-stroke engines the inlet valve opens just
(a) before t.d.c. and closes just after b.d.c.
(b) after t.d.c. and closes just before b.d.c.
(c) before b.d.c. and closes just after t.d.c.
(d) after b.d.c. and closes just before t.d.c.

17   On which of the following engines is a push-rod used to operate the valves?
(a) O.h.c.
(b) O.h.v. with side camshaft
(c) O.h.v. with overhead camshaft
(d) Side valve

18   The pressure in an engine cylinder is less than atmospheric pressure when the engine is performing the stroke called
(a) induction
(b) compression
(c) power
(d) exhaust

19   A crankshaft sprocket has 20 teeth and rotates at 3000 rev/min. The size and speed of the camshaft sprocket is
Size (teeth)	Speed (rev/min)
(a) 10	1500
(b) 10	6000
(c) 40	1500
(d) 40	6000

20   The advantage of a multi-cylinder engine over a single cylinder engine is that the former is
(a) easier to start
(b) simple to service
(c) smoother in operation
(d) shorter in length

21   When No. 1 piston of a four-cylinder, in-line, four-stroke engine is performing the power stroke, the No. 4 piston is on the stroke called
(a) induction
(b) compression
(c) power
(d) exhaust

22   The angle in degrees moved by the crankshaft of a four-cyinder engine between firing impulses is
(a) 90   (c) 360
(b) 180   (d) 720

23   To ensure that No. 1 valve of a four-cylinder, in-line engine is set in the position for checking the valve clearance the crankshaft is turned until
(a) No. 2 valve is open fully
(b) No. 2 valve is closed
(c) No. 8 valve is open fully
(d) No. 8 valve is closed

24   The two firing orders used on four-cylinder in-line engines are
(a) 1342 and 1423
(b) 1423 and 1324
(c) 1324 and 1243
(d) 1243 and 1342

25   A single cylinder two-stroke engine is rotating at 3000 rev/min. The number of power strokes per minute is
(a) 750   (c) 3000
(b) 1500   (d) 6000

26   What is happening below the piston of a two-stroke engine at the instant when the spark occurs?
(a) New gas is being compressed
(b) Transfer port has just opened
(c) New gas is flowing in through the inlet port
(d) Inlet port is closed and depression is being formed

27   How does the petrol–air mixture enter the cylinder of a two-stroke engine?
(a) The gas is pumped up the transfer port
(b) The depression 'draws' in the gas through the inlet port
(c) The exhaust gas in the crankcase drives out the new gas
(d) The upward moving piston pumps in the gas

28   As applied to petrol the chemically correct mixture is
(a) 12 parts of petrol to 1 part of air (by mass)
(b) 12 parts of air to 1 part of petrol (by mass)
(c) 15 parts of petrol to 1 part of air (by mass)
(d) 15 parts of air to 1 part of petrol (by mass)

29   One duty of an induction manifold is to
(a) atomize the fuel   (c) meter the fuel
(b) vaporize the fuel   (d) regulate the fuel

30   An engine should not be operated in a closed garage because
(a) exhaust gas is poisonous
(b) of the risk of an explosion
(c) the engine receives an incorrect mixture
(d) the engine is damaged if the gas cannot escape

31   Two effects which result from supplying an engine with a mixture of 12 parts of air to 1 part of petrol are
(a) high fuel consumption and 'dirty' exhaust products
(b) slow combustion and high power output
(c) low fuel consumption and 'sooty' exhaust gas
(d) slow combustion and low fuel consumption

32   The purpose of a carburettor choke tube is to
(a) decrease the air speed, and decrease the air pressure
(b) increase the air speed, and decrease the air pressure
(c) decrease the air speed, and increase the air pressure
(d) increase the air speed, and increase the air pressure

33   The reason why petrol flows from the float chamber to the venturi is because
(a) of the difference in pressure
(b) of the difference in levels
(c) the float level is higher
(d) the air sucks out the petrol

34   Which part of a carburettor shuts off the air supply to aid cold starting?

(a) Throttle   (c) Strangler
(b) Float   (d) Needle valve

35   The quantity of petrol–air mixture that enters the engine cylinder is regulated by the
(a) throttle   (c) strangler
(b) float   (d) needle valve

36   A compensation system is incorporated in a modern fixed-choke carburettor to prevent
(a) flooding at high speed
(b) richness at high speed
(c) weakness at high speed
(d) starvation at high speed

37   One effect of a punctured carburettor float is:
(a) weak mixture   (c) low petrol level
(b) petrol flooding   (d) high air/fuel ratio

38   One reason for richening the petrol–air mixture for cold starting is:
(a) fuel particles are smaller
(b) quantity of air is smaller
(c) cold engine does not vaporize fuel
(d) cold petrol will not flow through jet

39   The outlet of a carburettor slow running system is situated on the
(a) engine side of the throttle
(b) choke side of the throttle
(c) waist of the venturi
(d) intake side of the venturi

40   An engine is fitted with a variable choke carburettor. What is the effect on the choke air-speed and depression of increasing the engine speed
(a) air speed and depression are decreased
(b) air speed is increased, depression is decreased
(c) air speed is increased, depression is increased
(d) air speed and depression remain constant

41   The method used on a constant-vacuum carburettor to supply a suitable mixture for cold starting is:
(a) jet is lowered
(b) needle is lowered
(c) strangler is closed
(d) flap on air-intake is closed

42   The petrol flow from a constant-vacuum carburettor is increased when the engine load is increased by
(a) altering the petrol level
(b) intensifying the choke depression
(c) speeding-up the airflow over the jet
(d) causing a piston to raise a tapered needle

43   Two factors which would increase the voltage required to produce a spark at the sparking plug are
(a) wider electrode gap and higher cylinder pressure
(b) wider electrode gap and lower cylinder pressure

(c) narrower electrode gap and higher cylinder pressure

(d) narrower electrode gap and lower cylinder pressure

44   The part of an ignition system which transforms the voltage from 12V to more than 9000V is the

(a) coil
(b) distributor
(c) capacitor
(d) contact-breaker

45   The rotor arm of a coil-ignition system fitted to a four-cylinder four-stroke engine is driven at

(a) quarter engine speed
(b) half engine speed
(c) engine speed
(d) twice engine speed

46   The purpose of the capacitor in a coil-ignition system is to

(a) transform the voltage
(b) act as a mechanical switch
(c) prevent arcing at the contact-breaker
(d) direct the current to the appropriate plug

47   A spark occurs at the sparking plug when the contact-breaker of a coil-ignition system

(a) just opens
(b) just closes
(c) is fully opened
(d) is fully closed

48   Modern coil-ignition distributor units incorporate automatic advance devices. The mechanism which advances the spark to suit the engine speed is a type called

(a) volume control
(b) air bleed
(c) centrifugal
(d) vacuum

49   The gap of a sparking plug is adjusted by

(a) filing the centre electrode
(b) filing the earth electrode
(c) bending the centre electrode
(d) bending the earth electrode

50   A 'dirty' exhaust and intense diesel knock from a C.I. engine is caused by

(a) high cylinder temperatures
(b) poor fuel atomization
(c) supplying insufficient fuel to suit the air
(d) breaking up the injected fuel into very fine particles

51   During normal running, the necessary heat to ignite the fuel in a diesel engine is obtained by using

(a) heater plugs
(b) a manifold heater
(c) a high compression ratio
(d) an uncooled cylinder head

52   In a C.I. engine the fuel is injected when the piston

(a) is approaching t.d.c. at the end of the compression stroke
(b) has just passed t.d.c. at the start of the power stroke
(c) is approaching b.d.c. at the end of the induction stroke
(d) has just passed b.d.c. at the start of the compression stroke

53   Power output of a diesel engine is controlled by

(a) varying the pump timing
(b) varying the compression ratio
(c) regulating the quantity of air induced
(d) regulating the quantity of fuel injected

54   In the majority of two-stroke C.I. engines the induction charge of air is introduced by

(a) a blower
(b) a transfer port
(c) the depression caused by the downward moving piston
(d) the pressure difference between the atmosphere and the crankcase

55   The fins at the top of a motor cycle engine cylinder are longer than those at the bottom because

(a) hot air rises
(b) the top is the hottest part
(c) they are in an unexposed position
(d) extra strength is required at the top

56   Water circulation in a thermo-syphon cooling system is caused by

(a) conduction currents
(b) a belt driven water impeller
(c) a gear driven water pump
(d) the change in density of the water

57 The direction of the flow of water through the radiator of a thermo-syphon cooling system is from the
(a) top to the bottom   (c) front to the back
(b) bottom to the top   (d) back to the front

58 The main purpose of the fan of a liquid cooling system for an engine is to
(a) disperse engine fumes
(b) cool the external surfaces of the engine
(c) pump hot air over the cold cooling water
(d) give an airflow when the vehicle speed is low

59 The principle of a radiator of an engine cooling system is to
(a) act as a reservoir for the water
(b) cause a heat flow by convection currents
(c) spread out the hot water over a large area
(d) increase the air speed as it flows over the hot surface

60 Modern engines use a pump operated cooling system instead of the thermo-syphon system because the latter
(a) could not be pressurized
(b) overcooled the cylinder head and valves
(c) required a large quantity of water
(d) does not allow a thermostat to be fitted

61 The purpose of a thermostat in an engine cooling system is to
(a) prevent the coolant from boiling
(b) allow the engine to warm up quickly
(c) pressurize the system to raise the boiling point
(d) indicate to the driver the coolant temperature

62 Extra care must be taken when removing a modern radiator cap from a hot engine because
(a) the seal can be damaged
(b) of the risk of scalding
(c) the cooling system pressure is lower than atmospheric
(d) the sudden increase in pressure can damage the radiator

63 The purpose of adding an anti-freeze solution to the coolant is to
(a) prevent the coolant from freezing
(b) lower the freezing point of the coolant
(c) stop the formation of ice in the radiator
(d) avoid piston seizure due to ice in the water jacket

64 The thermostat is normally positioned in the cooling system between the
(a) header hose and radiator
(b) radiator and bottom hose
(c) bottom hose and engine water jacket
(d) engine water jacket and header hose

65 The purpose of the large spring loaded valve in a radiator cap is to
(a) lower the temperature at which the coolant boils
(b) prevent the coolant escaping when it boils
(c) reduce the risk of the rubber hoses collapsing when the pressure is low
(d) pressurize the system which raises the boiling-point of the coolant

66 The thermostat used in the majority of modern engine cooling systems is a type called
(a) wax   (c) bi-metal
(b) bellows   (d) alcohol

67 The quantity of anti-freeze in a cooling system is normally determined by measuring the
(a) relative density with a special hydrometer
(b) temperature at which the coolant boils
(c) temperature at which the coolant freezes
(d) pressure of the coolant at a temperature of 80°C

68 When comparing two oils of viscosities SAE 20 and SAE 40, which one has the highest viscosity and what is meant by 'viscosity'?
(a) SAE 20; viscosity means the density
(b) SAE 40; viscosity means the density
(c) SAE 20; viscosity means the thickness
(d) SAE 40; viscosity means the thickness

69 What term is used to describe the type of lubrication given to an engine piston?
(a) Boundary   (c) Pumped
(b) Pressure   (d) Full-film

70 A relief valve is fitted to the main oil gallery of an engine. The purpose of this valve is to
(a) limit the maximum oil pressure
(b) open when the oil is hot
(c) maintain the supply if the gallery becomes blocked
(d) stop the oil flow to the bearings when the pressure is low

3 The Transmission System

3.1 The Clutch

A transmission clutch performs two tasks:

1 it disengages the engine from the transmission to allow for gear changing,
2 it is a means for gradually engaging the engine to the driving wheels. When a vehicle is to be moved from rest the clutch must engage a stationary gearbox shaft with the engine; this must be rotating at a high speed to provide sufficient power or else the load will be too great and the engine will stall (come to rest).

The clutch used depends on the type of gearbox:

1 automatic gearboxes normally use a *fluid clutch*, which automatically disengages when the engine speed falls below about 800 rev/min,
2 manually operated gearboxes use a *dry friction clutch*.

Friction Clutches

A friction plate sandwiched between the engine flywheel and a spring loaded pressure plate transmits the drive to the gearbox: the extent of the drive is controlled by the force which is clamping the plate.

Lowering the driver's pedal causes disengagement by separating the friction surfaces: during this operation the force of the spring is taken by the driver. Initial upward movement of the pedal causes the friction surfaces to contact; further pedal movement allows the full spring force to act on the driven plate to ensure that all plates rotate at the same speed, i.e. no *slip*.

Types of friction clutch

Most friction clutches are of the 'dry' type, i.e. they do not run in oil. In fact if oil gets on the asbestos-based friction lining then the clutch will not operate correctly.

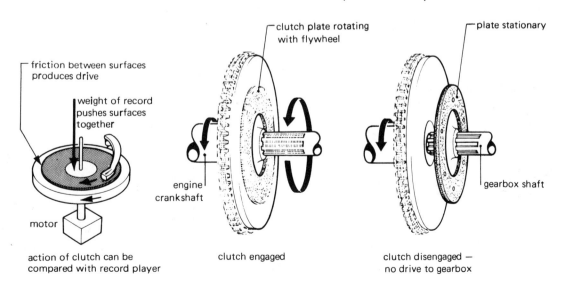

friction between surfaces produces drive

weight of record pushes surfaces together

motor

action of clutch can be compared with record player

clutch plate rotating with flywheel

engine crankshaft

clutch engaged

plate stationary

gearbox shaft

clutch disengaged — no drive to gearbox

Principle of friction clutch

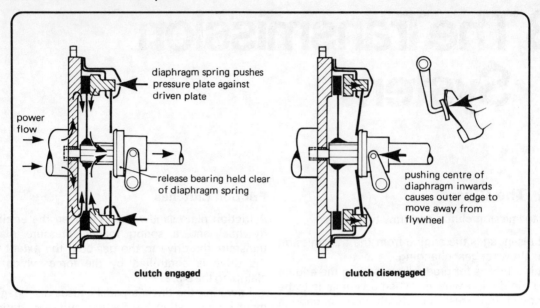

diaphragm spring pushes pressure plate against driven plate

power flow

release bearing held clear of diaphragm spring

clutch engaged

pushing centre of diaphragm inwards causes outer edge to move away from flywheel

clutch disengaged

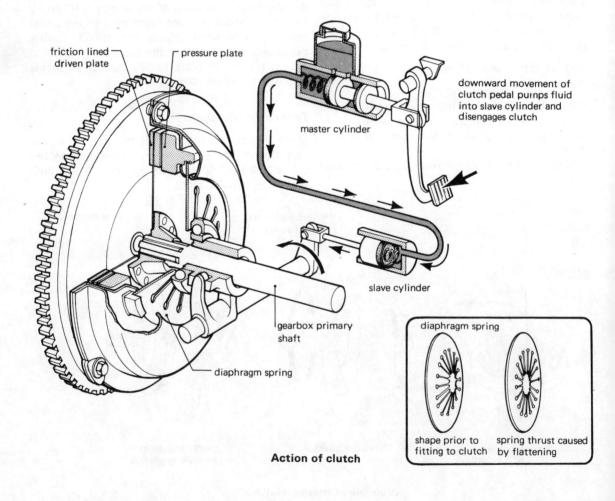

friction lined driven plate

pressure plate

master cylinder

downward movement of clutch pedal pumps fluid into slave cylinder and disengages clutch

slave cylinder

gearbox primary shaft

diaphragm spring

diaphragm spring

shape prior to fitting to clutch

spring thrust caused by flattening

Action of clutch

Most vehicles use a single-plate (one driven plate) type because this compact design is efficient especially as regards the disengagement: when new it does not suffer from *drag*, which is a term used to describe an incomplete disengagement.

On some vehicles, e.g. motor-cycles, a clutch of small diameter is necessary, so to balance this restriction more than one driven plate is used; the type is called multi-plate.

Pressure on the friction plate is obtained by using either a *diaphragm spring* or a *multi-spring* assembly; the former type is commonly used on cars. *Pedal linkage* between the pedal and the clutch is either *mechanical* or *hydraulic*. A small clearance in the linkage must be provided to ensure that the driven plate receives the full force of the spring or else slip will occur.

Clutch faults

The following are the main faults:

Slip – failure of the surfaces to grip resulting in the driven plate revolving slower than the engine flywheel: clutch gets hot and emits an odour.

Spin or drag – failure of the plates to separate resulting in noise from the gearbox when selecting a gear: most noticeable when the vehicle is stationary.

Judder – a vibration which occurs when the clutch is being engaged, i.e. when the drive is being taken up.

Fierceness – sudden departure of the vehicle even though the pedal is being released gradually.

3.2 The Gearbox

Besides providing for the forward or reverse motion of a vehicle the gearbox must overcome one of the drawbacks of the internal combustion engine: the poor torque output at low engine speeds. Gearing is provided either to:

1 boost the engine's torque output, or to
2 enable the engine to be operated at a speed where its output power is high.

Sliding-mesh Gearbox

Although this type is rarely used today, it is included because the gear layout forms the basic construction of most modern manual gearboxes.

The spur gears are mounted on three shafts:

1 primary (alternative names; clutch or first motion shaft),
2 layshaft (countershaft),
3 mainshaft (third motion shaft).

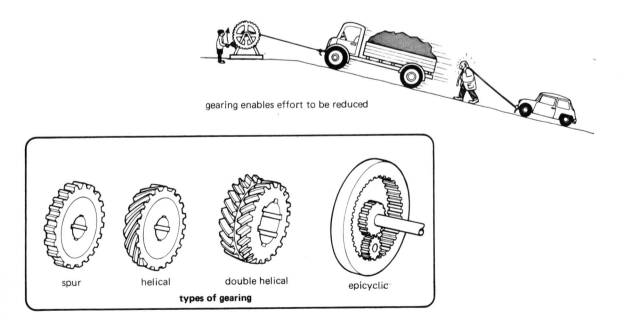

gearing enables effort to be reduced

| spur | helical | double helical | epicyclic |

types of gearing

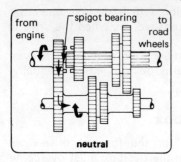

neutral

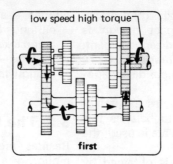

low speed high torque

first

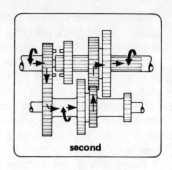

second

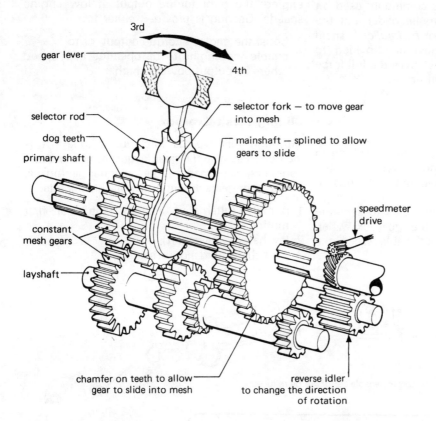

3rd

4th

gear lever

selector fork — to move gear into mesh

selector rod

dog teeth

mainshaft — splined to allow gears to slide

primary shaft

constant mesh gears

layshaft

speedmeter drive

chamfer on teeth to allow gear to slide into mesh

reverse idler to change the direction of rotation

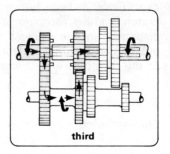

third

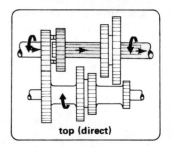

top (direct)

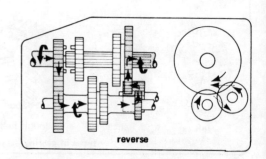

reverse

Four-speed sliding mesh gearbox

Manual	Manual	Gear is obtained by sliding a spur gear wheel into mesh with a pinion
	Constant-mesh	All gears are continually in mesh, gear selection obtained by using a dog clutch to lock the gear to the shaft
	Synchro-mesh	A constant-mesh layout having friction cones to equalize the speeds during gear-changing: this simplifies driving
Automatic	Torque converter and epicyclic gearbox	A fluid clutch, which provides a variable gear ratio, drives a three- or four-speed gearbox that changes automatically to suit engine and road conditions

Selector mechanism

This is the rod and lever arrangement fitted between the driver's gear lever and the gear wheels. The mechanism must include a means for:

1 holding the gear in position – generally a spring loaded ball,
2 preventing two gears being obtained at the same time – balls or plungers between the selector rods act as an interlock.

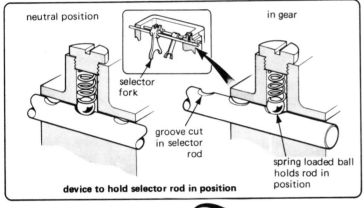

neutral position

in gear

selector fork

groove cut in selector rod

spring loaded ball holds rod in position

device to hold selector rod in position

Selector mechanism

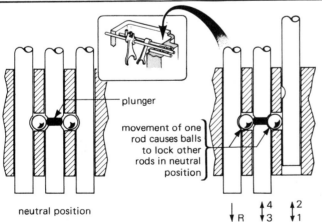

plunger

movement of one rod causes balls to lock other rods in neutral position

neutral position

R   4   2
     3   1

ball and plunger type of interlocking mechanism prevent two gears engaging at the same time

Operation	Effect on layshaft	Method
Changing up (e.g. first to second)	Slowed down	1 Depress clutch and shift lever to neutral 2 Release clutch, pause and depress clutch 3 Shift lever to higher gear and release clutch
Changing down	Speeded up	1 Release accelerator and depress clutch 2 Shift lever to neutral and release clutch 3 Accelerate engine 4 Depress clutch and shift lever to lever gear 5 Release clutch and accelerate

Gear changing

In the case of a sliding-mesh gearbox, gear changing demands skill if noise is to be avoided.

Crashing (or clashing) of the gears as the result of a bad change suggests the reason why this type is often called a 'crash' type gearbox.

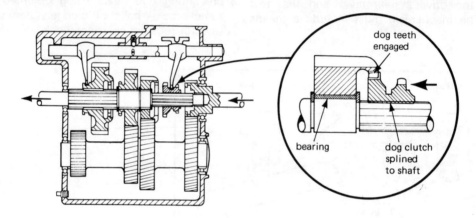

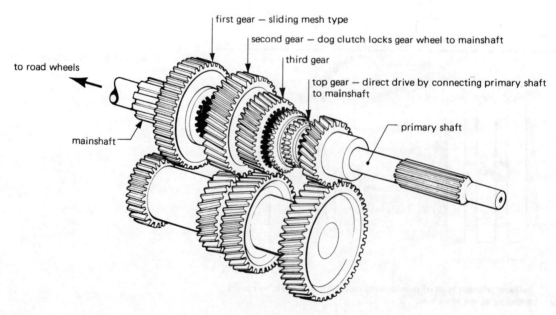

Constant-mesh gearbox

The operation *double declutching* must be performed by the driver if a quick and quiet change is required. This operation equalizes the peripheral (outside) speeds of the gears to be meshed.

A chamfer on the tooth allows for easier meshing but burrs will result from frequent bad changes.

Lubrication

This is provided by causing the layshaft gears to distribute the oil. The oil level is set about half way up the layshaft.

Constant-mesh Gearbox

This type uses helical or double helical gears which are always in mesh. The mainshaft gear wheels are mounted on bearings and when a gear is required the mainshaft gear is locked to the shaft by a dog clutch.

Although the mechanical efficiency is lower the helical gears are quieter and any damage resulting from a bad gear change occurs to the dog teeth instead of the actual gear teeth.

Synchro-mesh

As the name suggests this type has a synchronization device which equalizes the speeds of the two members that have to be meshed to obtain the gear.

The layout is similar to the constant-mesh but has friction cones fitted between the dog clutch and the gear wheel.

During gear selection the friction contact causes the layshaft to vary its speed so that both parts of the dog clutch are moving at the same speed when the actual locking of the gear takes place.

The operation of the friction device performs a duty which, in older designs, was carried out by the driver during double-declutching. The synchro-mesh gearbox gives a simpler, quieter and quicker gear change.

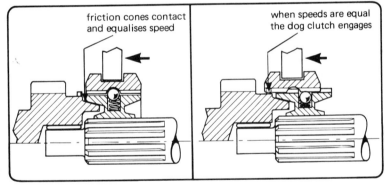

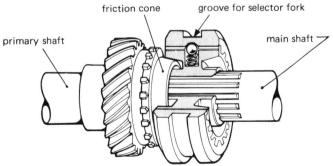

Principle of the synchro-mesh gearbox

3.3 Propeller Shafts and Universal Joints

Propeller Shafts

The propeller shaft transmits the drive from the gearbox mainshaft to the final drive pinion. The shaft is long so it is made of tubular section and balanced to reduce vibration.

A shaft connecting the final drive to an independently sprung driving road wheel is called a *drive shaft*: these are short in length so a solid shaft can be used for compactness.

Universal Joints

A universal joint is a device to transmit the drive through a varying angle.

Axle movement due to bumps in the road cause the distance between the gearbox and rear axle to alter; a sliding splined joint or flexibility within the joint must be provided to allow for this.

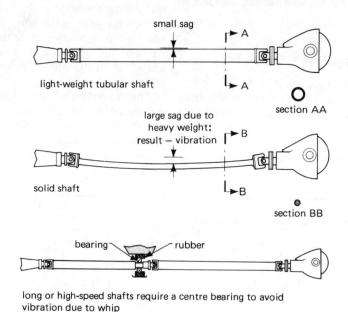

small sag

A

A

light-weight tubular shaft

section AA

large sag due to heavy weight: result — vibration

B

B

solid shaft

section BB

bearing — rubber

long or high-speed shafts require a centre bearing to avoid vibration due to whip

Propeller shafts

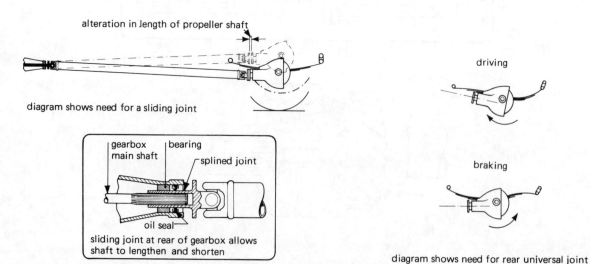

alteration in length of propeller shaft

diagram shows need for a sliding joint

driving

braking

gearbox main shaft | bearing
splined joint
oil seal
sliding joint at rear of gearbox allows shaft to lengthen and shorten

diagram shows need for rear universal joint

Rear axle movement

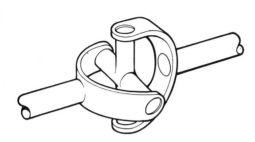

hooke type joint

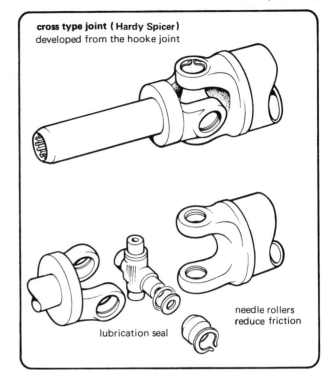

cross type joint (Hardy Spicer)
developed from the hooke joint

lubrication seal

needle rollers
reduce friction

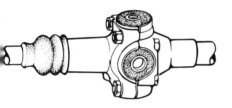

**cross type with rubber bushing
to absorb vibrations**

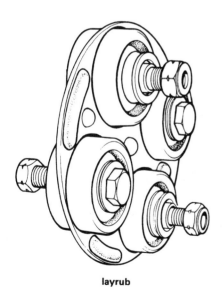

layrub

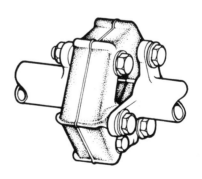

'doughnut' rubber coupling

Universal joints

Constant-velocity universal joint

Used at the road wheel end of the drive shaft of a front-wheel drive vehicle, this type of joint is capable of giving a smooth drive through a large drive angle.

A shaft which receives the drive from a Hooke type joint varies its speed during rotation; the greater the drive angle the greater the speed variation. A constant rotational speed can be restored by fitting a second joint in a way such that when the first joint increases its speed the second joint decreases its speed.

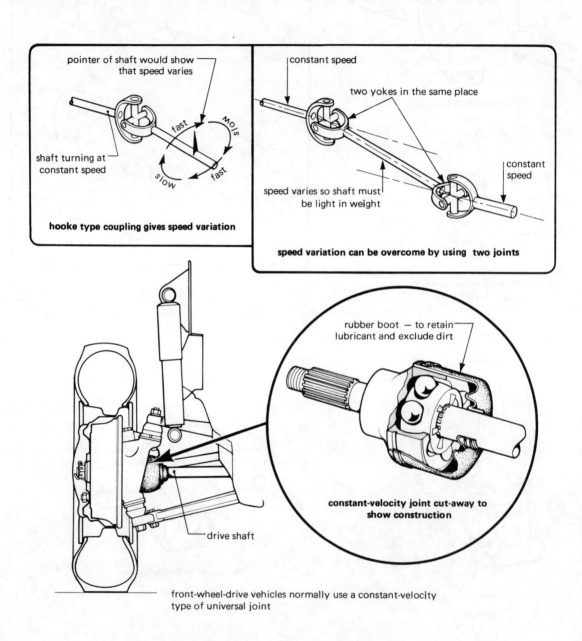

pointer of shaft would show that speed varies

shaft turning at constant speed

hooke type coupling gives speed variation

constant speed

two yokes in the same place

constant speed

speed varies so shaft must be light in weight

speed variation can be overcome by using two joints

rubber boot — to retain lubricant and exclude dirt

constant-velocity joint cut-away to show construction

drive shaft

front-wheel-drive vehicles normally use a constant-velocity type of universal joint

Arrangements to obtain constant velocity

3.4 Final Drive and Differential

A conventional transmission has a tubular rear axle to support the weight of the rear of the car. This axle contains the final drive gears, differential and axle shafts.

The Final Drive

To avoid loss of power the top gearbox ratio is 1:1, i.e. direct: this means that the propeller shaft rotates at engine speed. The duty of the final drive gears is to gear down the speed to suit the road wheels and to redirect the line of drive.

A crown wheel and pinion bevel gear having a gear ratio of about 4:1 is commonly used on cars but a lower ratio, e.g. 6:1, is necessary to suit the larger road wheels used on commercial vehicles.

Types of bevel gear

The hypoid gear is in common use today due mainly to the fact that the offset pinion allows the propeller shaft to be set below, (for cars) or above, (for commercial vehicles) the crown wheel centre. This gives either a reduction in the propeller shaft tunnel, which causes a bump in the vehicle floor, or in the case of a commercial vehicle a reduction in the angle through which the universal joint has to operate.

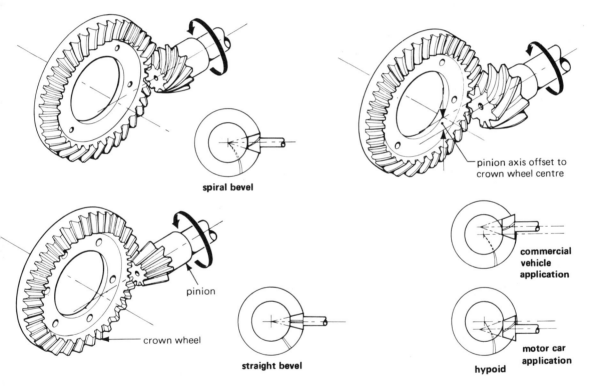

spiral bevel

pinion axis offset to crown wheel centre

commercial vehicle application

pinion

crown wheel

straight bevel

hypoid

motor car application

Type	Advantages	Disadvantages
Straight toothed bevel	High efficiency (low power losses) Cheap to produce	Noisy in operation
Spiral bevel	Quiet in operation	High tooth pressures
Hypoid	Propeller shaft can be set in a higher or lower position Very quiet Stronger pinion	Stronger bearings required Low efficiency Special lubricant needed to resist wear on teeth

The Differential

When a vehicle is cornered the inner wheel moves through a shorter distance than the outer wheel. This means that the inner wheel must slow down and the outer wheel must speed up. During this period it is desirable that each driving wheel maintains its driving action. The differential performs these two tasks.

Action of differential

The principle of the bevel type differential can be seen if the unit is considered as two discs and a lever.

When the vehicle is travelling straight, the lever will divide the driving force equally and both discs will move the same amount.

When the vehicle corners, the driving force will still be divided equally but the inner disc will now move through a smaller distance; this will cause the lever to pivot about its centre which will prize forward the outer disc to give it a greater movement. This action shows that the torque applied to each driving wheel is always equal — hence the differential is sometimes called a *torque equalizer*.

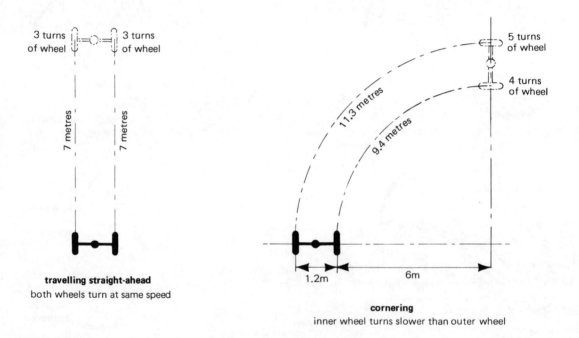

travelling straight-ahead
both wheels turn at same speed

cornering
inner wheel turns slower than outer wheel

Need for differential

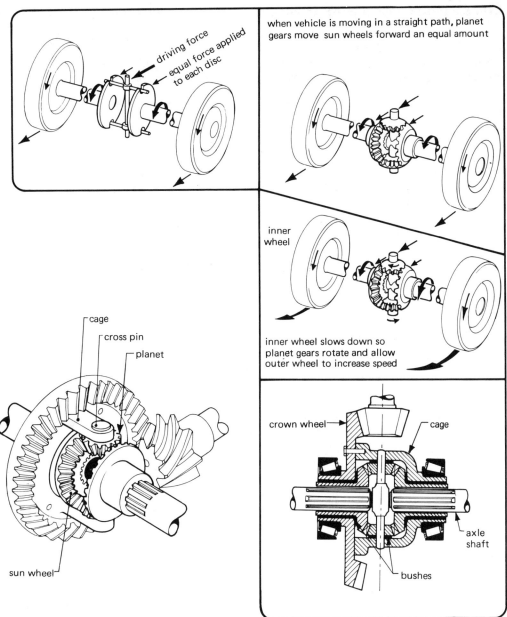

driving force

equal force applied to each disc

when vehicle is moving in a straight path, planet gears move sun wheels forward an equal amount

inner wheel

inner wheel slows down so planet gears rotate and allow outer wheel to increase speed

cage

cross pin

planet

sun wheel

crown wheel

cage

axle shaft

bushes

Action of differential

Axle Shaft and Rear Hub Arrangement

The axle shaft (half shaft) connects the differential sun wheel to the road wheel.

Most vehicles use a 'banjo' type of rear axle casing, so the axle shaft is splined to the differ-ential to allow the shaft to be withdrawn.

Rear hub construction

This governs the loads which have to be carried by the axle shaft.

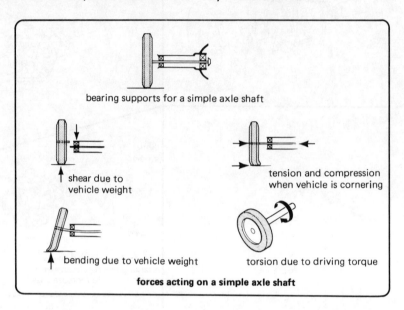

bearing supports for a simple axle shaft

shear due to vehicle weight

tension and compression when vehicle is cornering

bending due to vehicle weight

torsion due to driving torque

forces acting on a simple axle shaft

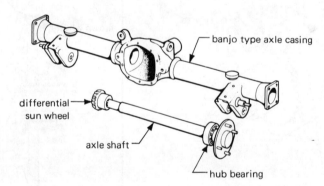

banjo type axle casing

differential sun wheel

axle shaft

hub bearing

Type of hub	Hub bearing arrangement	Stresses which act on shaft	Application
Semi-floating	Single bearing between shaft and casing	1 Torsional 2 Bending 3 Shear 4 Tension and compression	Cars
Three-quarter floating	Single bearing between hub and casing	1 Torsional 2 Slight bending	Cars
Fully floating	Two bearings widely spaced between hub and casing	1 Torsional	Commercial vehicles

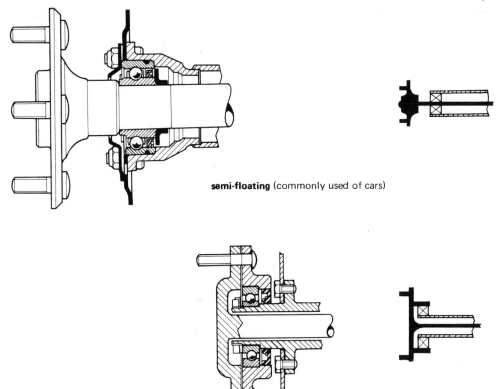

semi-floating (commonly used of cars)

three-quarter floating (rarely used today)

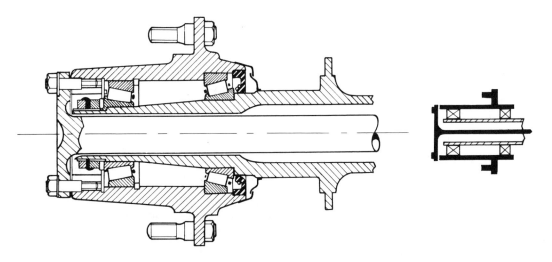

fully-floating (commonly used on heavy vehicles)

Rear hub construction

3.5 Review Questions

1 Most vehicles having automatic transmission connect the engine to the gearbox by means of a
(a) dog clutch
(b) fluid clutch
(c) dry friction clutch
(d) wet friction clutch

2 The common type of clutch fitted between the engine and a synchro-mesh gearbox is called a
(a) dog
(b) cone
(c) multi-plate
(d) dry friction

3 What causes the main force which opposes the driver when the clutch pedal is depressed?
(a) The thrust springs
(b) The speed of rotation
(c) The friction in the linkage
(d) The friction between the linings

4 The action which takes place in the clutch when the pedal is depressed is:
(a) pressure plate comes to rest
(b) pressure plate moves away from the flywheel
(c) driven plate moves towards the flywheel
(d) driven plate slows down to flywheel speed

5 Clutch slip could be caused by
(a) excessive clearance at pedal
(b) seizure of the spigot bearing
(c) lack of clearance in pedal linkage
(d) excessive friction between lining and flywheel

6 Which one of the following applies to a single-plate clutch?

	Number of driven plates	Number of driving surfaces
(a)	1	1
(b)	1	2
(c)	2	1
(d)	2	2

7 The clamping force on the linings of a single-plate clutch is given by a
(a) pneumatic cylinder
(b) hydraulic cylinder
(c) diaphragm spring
(d) single helical spring

8 The symptom of 'failure of the clutch plates to separate' is
(a) odour emitted from clutch
(b) vibration when the vehicle moves off
(c) difficulty in obtaining first gear without noise
(d) noise when the engine is pulling hard

9 One reason for fitting a gearbox is to overcome one of the drawbacks of the I.C. engine, namely the
(a) low torque at low speed
(b) high torque at low speed
(c) low power at high speed
(d) high power at low speed

10 The gears in a constant-mesh gearbox have teeth which are inclined to the shaft axis. This type of gear is called
(a) spur
(b) worm
(c) bevel
(d) helical

11 To which gearbox type does the following statement apply? 'Dog clutches are used to obtain the gears and double declutching is necessary.'
(a) Crash type
(b) Sliding-mesh
(c) Constant-mesh
(d) Synchro-mesh

12 The speedometer is driven from the gearbox shaft called
(a) primary
(b) lay
(c) counter
(d) main

13 A bearing noise is heard when the engine is running and the vehicle is stationary but the noise ceases when the clutch is disengaged. A possible cause is a defective
(a) clutch release bearing
(b) clutch spigot bearing
(c) primary shaft bearing
(d) main shaft rear bearing

14 The purpose of double declutching when changing down is to
(a) slow down the layshaft
(b) speed up the layshaft
(c) slow down the mainshaft
(d) speed up the mainshaft

15 An engine rotating at 1000 rev/min drives through a gearbox set in first gear. If the ratio is 4:1 the mainshaft speed and direction, relative to the engine, is

	Speed (rev/min)	Direction
(a)	250	same
(b)	250	opposite
(c)	4000	same
(d)	4000	opposite

16 The purpose of the interlocking plungers fitted between the gearbox selector rods is:
(a) stops the gear jumping out of mesh
(b) holds the gear in the engaged position
(c) resists reverse being engaged when the vehicle is moving forward
(d) prevents two gears being obtained at the same time

17 In a sliding-mesh gearbox a small gear transfers the drive from a layshaft pinion to a mainshaft wheel. The purpose of this small gear is to
(a) drive the speedometer
(b) obtain direct drive
(c) lubricate the spigot
(d) provide reverse motion

18 Direct drive in a gearbox is generally obtained by connecting
(a) together two gears of equal size
(b) the smallest mainshaft gear to the mainshaft
(c) the smallest layshaft pinion with the largest mainshaft wheel
(d) the primary shaft to the mainshaft by a dog clutch

19 Lubrication of a manual type gearbox is achieved by
(a) submerging all gears in oil
(b) immersing the layshaft in oil
(c) connecting the oilways to the engine pump
(d) a pressure pump driven from the input shaft

20 Which one of the following gearbox types uses friction cones to equalize the speeds of the members prior to gear engagement?
(a) Crash type
(b) Sliding-mesh
(c) Constant-mesh
(d) Synchro-mesh

21 A propeller shaft is tubular instead of solid because
(a) a solid shaft is weaker
(b) its sag is smaller
(c) it is more rigid
(d) it resists 'wind-up'

22 The purpose of the sliding joint at the front end of a propeller shaft is to allow
(a) the shaft to be removed and refitted
(b) the drive to be transmitted through a varying angle
(c) for the change in distance between the gearbox and axle
(d) for the variation in speed of the front universal joint

23 A universal joint which is constructed with two yokes joined by a cross-shaped trunnion is a type called
(a) Hookes
(b) Layrub
(c) doughnut
(d) constant-velocity

24 A constant-velocity universal joint is used at the
(a) front end of the propeller shaft
(b) rear end of the propeller shaft
(c) road wheel end of the shaft on front-wheel drive vehicles
(d) differential end of the shaft on front-wheel drive vehicle

25 The crown wheel and pinion is called the
(a) differential
(b) rear axle
(c) final drive
(d) rear drive

26   In error the final drive assembly was fitted upside-down in the rear axle such that the crown wheel is now on the right-hand-side of the pinion. The effect of this error is:
(a) the propeller shaft will rotate in the opposite direction
(b) the direction of rotation of the road wheels is reversed
(c) one half-shaft will turn forwards the other will turn backwards
(d) the inner wheel will be speeded up, the outer will be slowed down

27   Compared with the normal type of spiral bevel gear, a hypoid gear has the advantage:
(a) higher efficiency
(b) cheaper to produce
(c) weaker bearings can be used on the pinion
(d) higher or lower propeller shaft can be used

28   When a vehicle turns a corner, the action of the differential causes
(a) the inner wheel to speed up
(b) the outer wheel to speed up
(c) an increase in the torque applied to the inner wheel
(d) an increase in the torque applied to the outer wheel

29   When a vehicle is cornering the crown wheel is rotating at 500 rev/min and the outer wheel is turning at 520 rev/min. The speed of the inner wheel is
(a) 20 rev/min
(b) 480 rev/min
(c) 500 rev/min
(d) 540 rev/min

30   The type of hub used on a heavy commercial vehicle is a
(a) quarter-floating
(b) semi-floating
(c) three-quarter floating
(d) fully floating

4 Suspension, and Body Construction

4.1 Springs and Dampers

Road springs and suspension dampers are needed to cushion and damp out the road shocks so as to give comfort to the vehicle occupants and prevent damage to the components.

Road Springs

A spring fitted between the wheel and the vehicle body allows the wheel to follow the road surface with the minimum disturbance to the body.

Various forms of springing are used; these include

1 steel — laminated, helical and torsion bar,
2 rubber,
3 pneumatic.

Laminated or Leaf Spring

A cheap system which not only acts as a spring but also locates the axle.

To overcome weakness at the mid-point of the main leaf, either the leaf is made thicker at the centre or a series of leaves is used. A spring having many leaves gives a harsh ride due to the friction between the leaves.

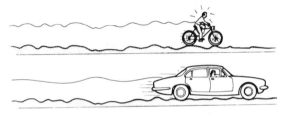

Springs reduce vertical oscillations

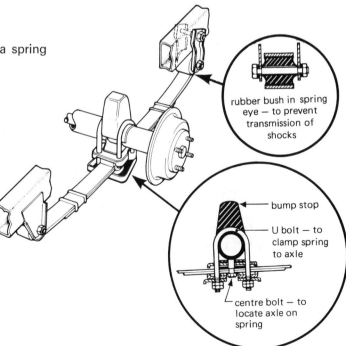

rubber bush in spring eye — to prevent transmission of shocks

bump stop

U bolt — to clamp spring to axle

centre bolt — to locate axle on spring

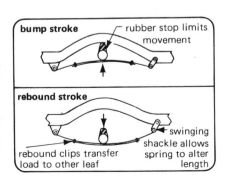

bump stroke

rubber stop limits movement

rebound stroke

rebound clips transfer load to other leaf

swinging shackle allows spring to alter length

Laminated or leaf spring

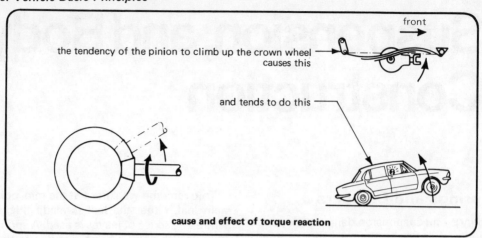

front

the tendency of the pinion to climb up the crown wheel
causes this

and tends to do this

cause and effect of torque reaction

Hotchkiss open

type drive

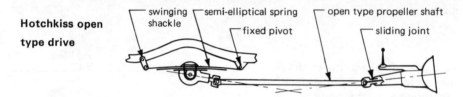

swinging
shackle — semi-elliptical spring — open type propeller shaft

fixed pivot — sliding joint

Hotchkiss or open type drive

This uses leaf springs to transfer the *driving thrust* from the axle to the vehicle frame. Also the springs take the *torque* reaction (tendency of the axle casing to rotate in the opposite direction to the road wheel).

Helical Spring

A popular spring which gives a smoother ride than the multi-leaf spring due to the absence of interleaf friction.

Many front and rear independent suspension systems use this type of spring.

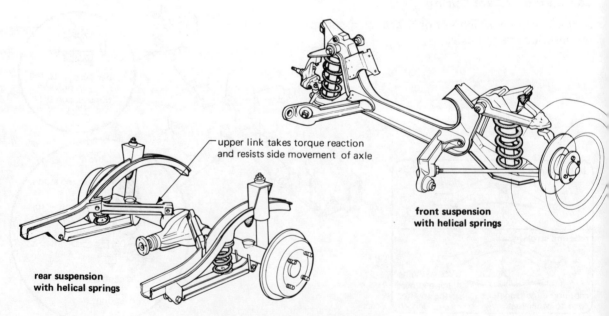

upper link takes torque reaction
and resists side movement of axle

**front suspension
with helical springs**

**rear suspension
with helical springs**

Helical spring suspension systems

Other Forms of Springing

Torsion bar, air and rubber springs are normally used in conjunction with independent suspension. Air and rubber springs are sometimes used on heavy commercial vehicles to assist the leaf springs when the vehicle is loaded.

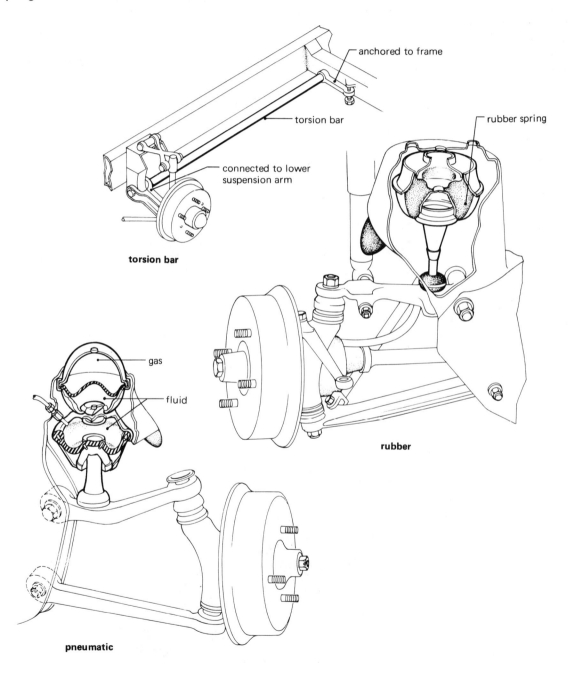

anchored to frame

torsion bar

connected to lower suspension arm

rubber spring

torsion bar

gas

fluid

rubber

pneumatic

Other types of spring

Dampers

When a spring is compressed and then released it will oscillate for a period of time before coming to rest. Applied to a vehicle this action will cause a most uncomfortable ride.

The purpose of a damper (often misleadingly called a shock absorber) is to absorb the energy stored in the spring and so reduce the time that the vehicle is bouncing.

Most modern dampers are hydraulic: they dissipate the energy by pumping oil through small orifices.

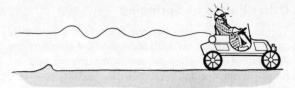

without damper — spring oscillates for a long time

with damper — oscillation ceases after a short time

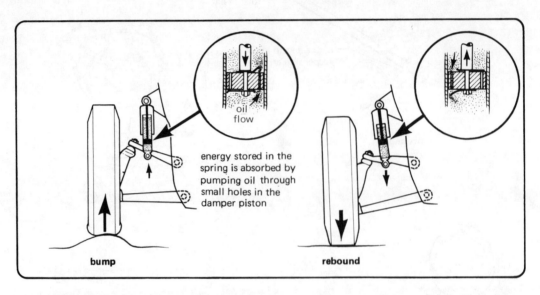

oil flow

energy stored in the spring is absorbed by pumping oil through small holes in the damper piston

bump

rebound

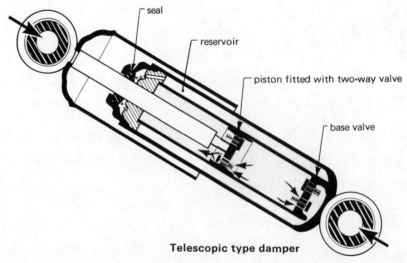

seal

reservoir

piston fitted with two-way valve

base valve

Telescopic type damper

4.2 Independent Suspension

Independent suspension is a system whereby the movement of one wheel has no effect on the other wheels. When applied to the front it is called independent front suspension (i.f.s.); many cars also have independent rear suspension (i.r.s.)

Cars have i.f.s. instead of a beam axle for the following reasons:

1 softer springing can be fitted,
2 steering is improved,
3 road wheel stays in contact with the road even if the surface is bumpy (i.e. the unsprung weight is lower),
4 engine can be mounted nearer the front of the vehicle so vehicle occupants obtain a better ride.

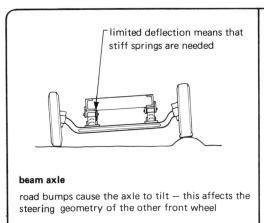

beam axle

road bumps cause the axle to tilt — this affects the steering geometry of the other front wheel

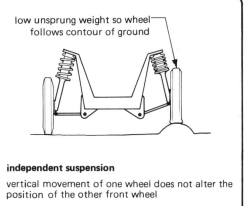

independent suspension

vertical movement of one wheel does not alter the position of the other front wheel

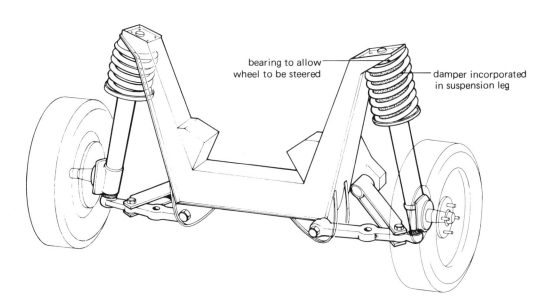

Independent suspension system

4.3 Wheels and Tyres

To maintain grip when a vehicle is travelling at speed over a bumpy surface, a wheel must be light in weight. Also it must be strong, cheap to produce, easy to clean and simple to remove.

Car Wheels

Three basic types of bolt on wheel are used:

1 pressed steel disc – rolled steel rim welded to a centre disc,
2 wire – rim attached to hub by wire spokes to give a lightweight wheel,
3 light alloy – a lightweight sports car wheel which is cast and machined.

These wheels all have well-based rim: this rim has a drop centre to allow for tyre removal; when the tyre bead opposite the valve is pushed into the well it allows the tyre to be levered over the edge of the rim.

Commercial Vehicle Wheels

The large tyre bead used for heavy vehicles requires a rim which has either a removable side flange or is divided at the centre.

Safety precautions

The 'explosion' caused by a damaged or incorrectly fitted rim flange can be fatal to the mechanic inflating the tyre. After fitting the flange to a commercial vehicle rim, the tyre should be placed in a steel cage whilst it is being inflated.

Fatal accidents have also occurred when the outer ring of nuts of a divided wheel were removed during a wheel change. These nuts should be painted red.

Tyres

Most cars use a *tubeless* type of tyre which has a soft rubber liner on the inside of the tyre: this membrane is carried over the bead to form an airtight seal on the wheel rim. Compared to the *tubed* type of tyre, the tubeless type has the advantage: slow deflation when it is punctured.

There are two basic forms of tyre construction:

1 cross ply,
2 radial ply.

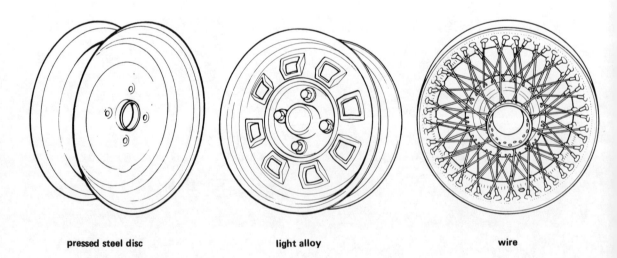

pressed steel disc   light alloy   wire

Car wheels

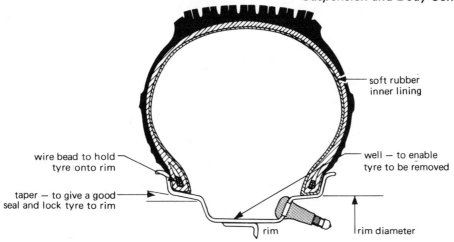

soft rubber
inner lining

wire bead to hold
tyre onto rim

well — to enable
tyre to be removed

taper — to give a good
seal and lock tyre to rim

rim

rim diameter

well base rim (fitted with tubeless type)

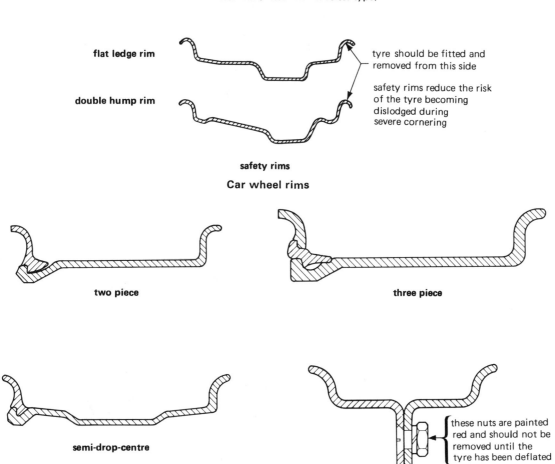

flat ledge rim

tyre should be fitted and
removed from this side

double hump rim

safety rims reduce the risk
of the tyre becoming
dislodged during
severe cornering

safety rims

Car wheel rims

two piece

three piece

semi-drop-centre

these nuts are painted
red and should not be
removed until the
tyre has been deflated

divided

Commercial vehicle wheel rims

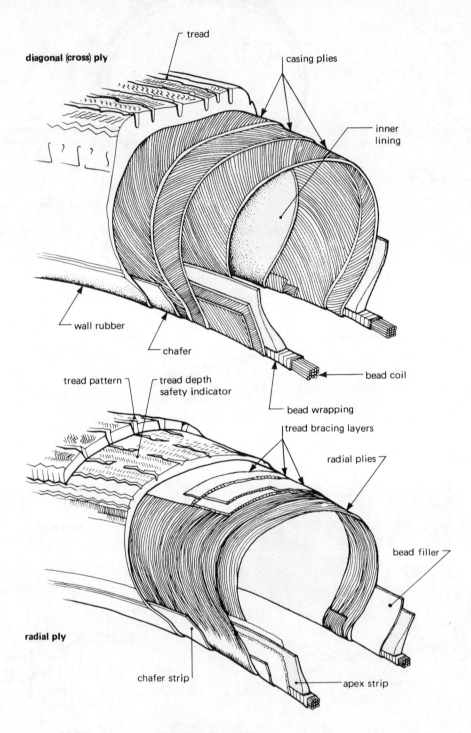

diagonal (cross) ply

tread

casing plies

inner lining

wall rubber

chafer

bead coil

tread pattern

tread depth safety indicator

bead wrapping

tread bracing layers

radial plies

bead filler

radial ply

chafer strip

apex strip

Tyre construction

A radial-ply tyre has the section width given in millimetres and is identified either by the word 'radial' moulded on the side wall or by the letter 'R' shown between the two size figures e.g. 185R380.

In the past, diagonal-ply tyre sizes have been stated in inches:

5·20–13 is a car tyre of width 5·2 in and rim diameter 13 in;

10·00–20 is a heavy vehicle tyre of width 10 in and rim diameter 20 in.

It is recommended that radial- and diagonal-ply tyres should not be 'mixed' on cars and light vans. When both types are used on a vehicle the law requires that:

1 tyres must not be mixed on the same axle,
2 radial-ply tyres are fitted to the rear and cross-ply tyres go to the front.

Failure to observe these regulations can result in a dangerous vehicle handling condition called *oversteer*: when the vehicle is cornered the rear drifts out and causes the vehicle to turn more sharply than intended.

Legal regulations

In these are listed various faults which make a tyre defective. It is dangerous and illegal to use a tyre that is:

1 unsuitable for the vehicle,
2 not properly inflated,
3 cut more than 25 mm (1 in) in length and of a depth which reaches the cords,
4 containing lumps or bulges,
5 exposing any cords,
6 worn to a tread depth less than 1 mm.

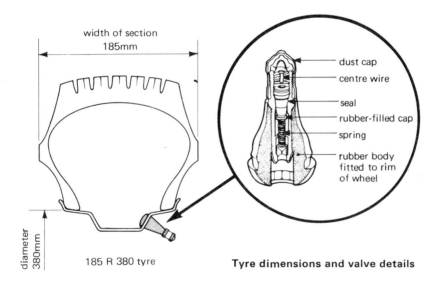

Tyre dimensions and valve details

Type	Advantages
Diagonal-ply tyre	1 Lighter steering at low speed 2 Not so critical in respect to steering geometry 3 Smoother ride at low speeds 4 Cheaper
Radial-ply tyre	1 About 80% longer life 2 Lower rolling resistance, so fuel consumption is improved 3 Side deflection is reduced so vehicle corners without 'drifting' 4 Full width of tread is held on the road when the vehicle is cornering, so grip is improved especially on wet roads

4.4 Body Construction

Chassis Frames

A separate chassis frame must be light yet strong enough to resist the various loads and road forces.

Car frames

Car frames are *inswept* at the front to allow the front wheels to be steered and *upswept* at the rear to allow clearance for the axle to move upwards when the wheels strike a bump. A separate car frame normally relies on the body to stiffen the construction.

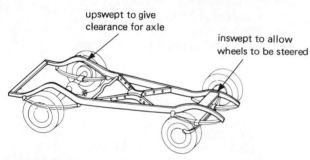

frame for beam axle system

(this obsolete design shows a disadvantage of a beam type front axle — the engine must be placed well back to give clearance for the axle)

upswept to give clearance for axle

inswept to allow wheels to be steered

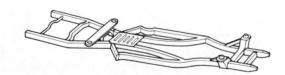

frame for vehicle having independent suspension

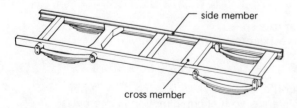

side member

cross member

frame for a commercial vehicle

Commercial vehicle frames

These normally consist of two long side members of channel section which are joined together by a number of cross members. Rubber mountings on the cab and main components reduce the transmission of vibration.

Frame sections

A thin flat bar of metal offers very little resistance to bending and twisting, so in order to obtain great strength from the minimum weight, the metal is formed into a channel, tubular or box section.

The Body Shell

The body used on most cars is a type called *integral* or *frameless*. This stiff all-steel body construction has the main components bolted directly onto it, so the absence of a separate frame results in a lightweight vehicle which is suitable for mass production.

Although the engine position, number of seats and size of boot dictates the basic body form, the final shape and style is governed by the appeal it has to the buying public.

Frame and Body Maintenance

Maintenance of the body is carried out to enhance its appearance and to resist the formation of rust. This type of corrosion occurs when:

1 bare steel comes into contact with air or water,

2 two dissimilar pieces of bare metal are joined by water.

In the second case the action is similar to a battery; the passage of electrical energy from one 'plate' to the other 'plate' erodes (eats away) the metal. Salt, mixed with the moisture that connects the two metals, increases the electrical flow, so this is why corrosion is accelerated when winter conditions make road salting necessary.

Paint, sealing compounds, and metallic plating such as chromium are used by the manufacturers to act as a barrier to protect the metal, therefore periodic attention should be given to ensure that these surface treatments continue to be effective.

Frame	Section	Behaviour
Flat	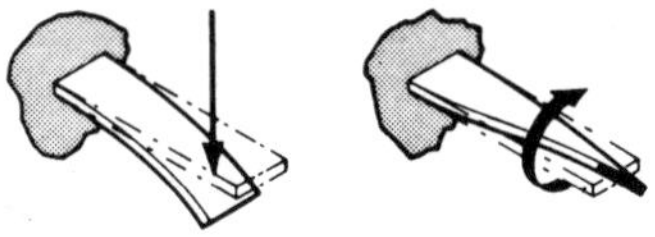	Offers little resistance to bending and twisting
Channel	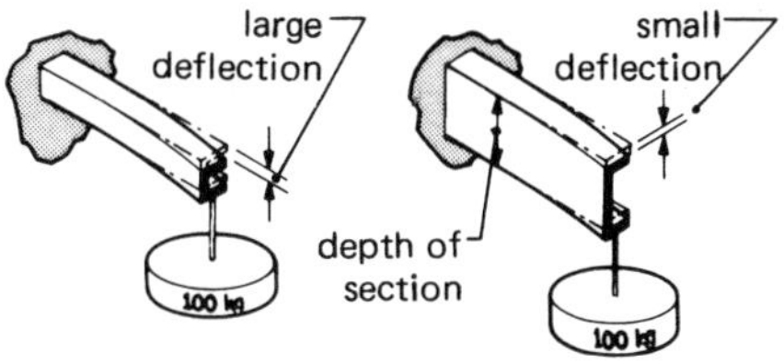 large deflection / small deflection / depth of section / 100 kg	Excellent resistance to bending. Resistance increases as depth of section is increased
Tubular		Excellent resistance to torsion. Resistance increases as diameter is increased
Box	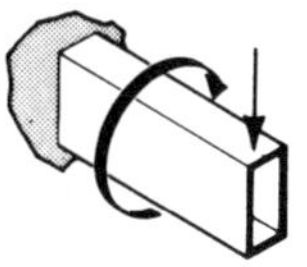	Good resistance to both bending and torsion

Routine maintenance should include the following:

Washing

Road grit and mud should be removed by frequent washing of the paintwork. Very careful attention should be given to out-of-sight areas such as beneath the sills, bottom of door jambs and other places where corrosion starts.

Polishing

Periodic wax polishing protects the paintwork and improves the appearance. Brightwork should also be polished to seal the small scratches.

Water drain holes

Dirt should be removed from the drain holes which are drilled in the bottom of the doors and other places which collect water.

Paintwork repairs

Deep scratches in the paintwork should be sealed with paint. In areas which have rusted the corrosion should be ground out, treated with an anti-rust compound and repainted.

Underseal repairs

An underseal compound should be applied to any places where the original treatment has become damaged. Special attention should be given to ensure that all metal joints are coated with underseal. Underseal compound must not contact the exhaust system.

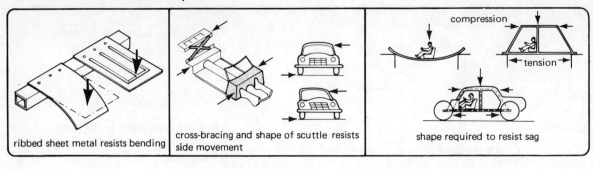

ribbed sheet metal resists bending

cross-bracing and shape of scuttle resists side movement

compression

tension

shape required to resist sag

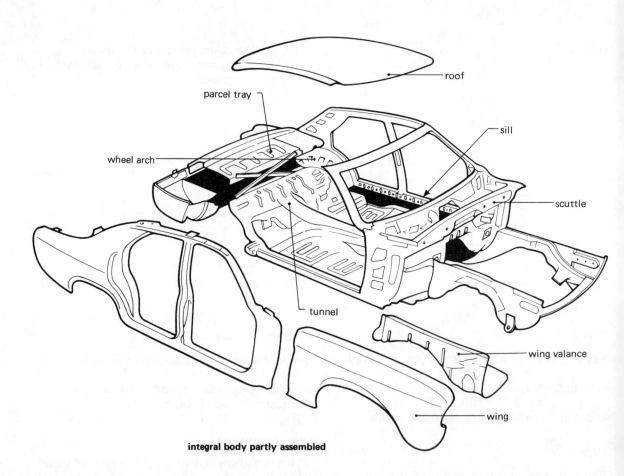

roof

parcel tray

sill

wheel arch

scuttle

tunnel

wing valance

wing

integral body partly assembled

4.5 Review Questions

1 Which one of the following suspension springs also acts as a means for locating the axle?
(a) Laminated
(b) Helical
(c) Torsion bar
(d) Rubber

2 The reason why a laminated spring is made up of a series of leaves is to
(a) reduce interleaf friction
(b) soften the spring action and increase the maximum deflection
(c) allow the leaves to slide during the bump movement
(d) overcome the weakness at the centre of a single leaf spring

3 An axle is located on a leaf spring by a
(a) U bolt
(b) spring clip
(c) centre bolt
(d) shackle pin

4 During the rebound stroke, the load is transmitted from the main leaf from the shorter leaves by a
(a) U bolt
(b) spring clip
(c) centre bolt
(d) shackle pin

5 Driving thrust and torque reaction is taken in a Hotchkiss type drive by the
(a) road springs
(b) radius rods
(c) swinging shackle
(d) propeller shaft

6 The provision made to allow a leaf spring to vary its length is a
(a) swinging shackle
(b) rubber U bolt mounting
(c) sliding centre bolt
(d) spline in the spring eye

7 The abbreviation used to describe a suspension arrangement in which the 'bump' movement of one rear wheel has no effect on the other rear wheel is
(a) i.m.s.   (c) i.n.s.
(b) i.f.s.   (d) i.r.s.

8 Two advantages of i.f.s. compared with a beam axle are:
(a) lower unsprung weight and softer springing can be used
(b) higher unsprung weight and softer springing can be used
(c) lower unsprung weight and harder springing can be used
(d) higher unsprung weight and harder springing can be used

9 The purpose of a suspension damper is to
(a) resist the road shocks
(b) reduce the 'bump' stroke of the spring
(c) transmit spring movement to the body
(d) absorb the energy stored in the spring

10 The purpose of the 'well' in a wheel rim is to
(a) lock the tyre onto the rim
(b) allow the tyre to be fitted and removed
(c) expose the valve of the inner tube
(d) prevent the tyre dislodging during severe cornering

11 What safety precaution should be taken when a tyre having a removeable side flange is initially inflated after fitting to the rim?
The tyre should be inflated
(a) in a steel cage
(b) with the flange towards the operator
(c) very slowly to allow the heat to dissipate
(d) slowly and allowed to stand for a period of time

12 What type of tyre has a slow deflation when punctured and offers a considerable resistance to side deflection when the vehicle is cornered?
(a) Tubed cross-ply
(b) Tubed radial-ply
(c) Tubeless cross-ply
(d) Tubeless radial-ply

13 The information given by the tyre marking 185R380 is:
(a) rayon tyre of width 185 mm and rim diameter of 380 mm
(b) rayon tyre of width 380 mm and rim radius of 185 mm
(c) radial-ply tyre of width 185 mm and rim diameter of 380 mm
(d) radial-ply tyre of width 380 mm and rim radius of 185 mm

14   As applied to a car, which one of the following tyre arrangements is dangerous and illegal?

	Front	Rear
(a)	Cross-ply	Cross-ply
(b)	Cross-ply	Radial-ply
(c)	Radial-ply	Radial-ply
(d)	Radial-ply	Cross-ply

15   Compared with a radial-ply tyre, one advantage of a cross-ply tyre is:
(a) longer life
(b) lower rolling resistance
(c) smoother ride at low speeds
(d) full width of tread held on road when vehicle is cornering

16   A chassis frame used on a car is inswept at the front and unswept at the rear to provide clearance for

	Front	Rear
(a)	engine sump	final drive housing
(b)	engine mountings	rear passenger seats
(c)	wheels to be steered	axle to move vertically
(d)	vertical wheel deflection	wheel movement

17   Which one of the following frame sections offers the least resistance to bending and twisting?
(a) Flat
(b) Channel
(c) Tubular
(d) Box

18   Which one of the following sections offers the highest resistance to torsion?
(a) Flat   (c) Tubular
(b) Channel   (d) Box

19   Which one of the following parts of an integral body acts as a compression member?
(a) Sill   (c) Floor
(b) Roof   (d) Tunnel

20   Paint reduces corrosion of a steel body panel by
(a) giving a surface which can be polished
(b) smoothing the porous surfaces which trap water
(c) acting as a barrier between the air and the steel
(d) causing a flow of electricity between the steel body parts

5 Steering and Braking Systems

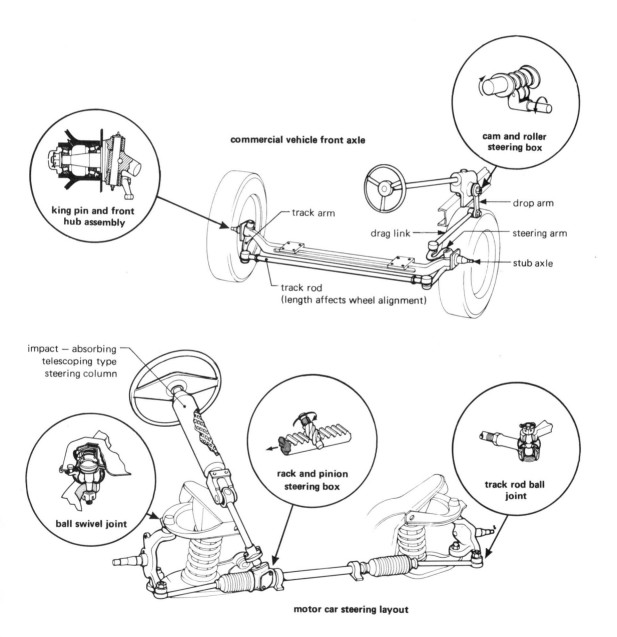

commercial vehicle front axle

king pin and front hub assembly

cam and roller steering box

track arm

drop arm

drag link

steering arm

stub axle

track rod
(length affects wheel alignment)

impact – absorbing
telescoping type
steering column

ball swivel joint

rack and pinion steering box

track rod ball joint

motor car steering layout

5.1 The Steering System

The type of steering layout depends on the suspension system. The beam axle used on heavy commercial vehicles has a king pin fitted at each end of the axle and this pin is the pivot which allows the wheels to be steered.

Cars have independent suspension and this system has ball joints to allow for wheel movement.

Steering Box

The steering box converts the rotary motion of the steering wheel to a reciprocating (backward and forward) motion. Also the box has gearing which reduces the effort applied by the driver. The mechanism between the steering box and steering wheel should collapse if the vehicle is involved in a collision.

Power-assisted Steering

To overcome the need and drawback of having a steering box with a low ratio, many heavy motor cars have a power-assisted steering (P.A.S.). These systems use hydraulic power to help the driver turn the road wheels when the steering load exceeds a given amount. The hydraulic pump is normally belt driven from the engine crankshaft.

Steering Geometry

When a vehicle turns a corner it rotates about an imaginary point called the *instantaneous centre of rotation*. To minimize tyre wear the front wheels should be steered from the straight ahead to:

a position where they form an angle of 90° to a line drawn from the instantaneous centre to the wheel centre.

A swinging beam is unsuitable for a modern vehicle so a stub axle pivots about a king pin or ball joint to give steering movement. This arrangement requires the steering linkage to:

turn the inner wheel through a larger angle than the outer wheel.

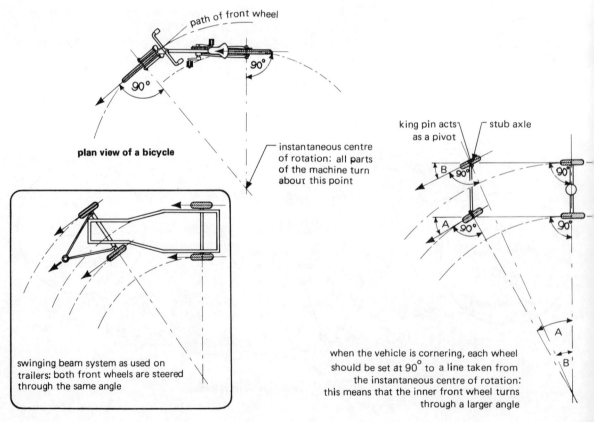

path of front wheel

90°

90°

plan view of a bicycle

instantaneous centre of rotation: all parts of the machine turn about this point

swinging beam system as used on trailers; both front wheels are steered through the same angle

king pin acts as a pivot — stub axle

B 90°

90°

A 90°

90°

A

B

when the vehicle is cornering, each wheel should be set at 90° to a line taken from the instantaneous centre of rotation: this means that the inner front wheel turns through a larger angle

The difference between the two steered angles is governed by the amount that the steering wheel is turned; the more the steering wheel is turned, the greater is the difference in angle. Also the angle difference depends on the ratio: track/wheelbase of a vehicle.

Ackermann layout

This layout is the common arrangement used to steer each front wheel through an angle which is similar to that which is required.

It is obtained by making the track rod a different length to the distance between the king pins (or wheel swivel axis centres). The track rod length is set so that its connection to the track arm falls on an imaginary line taken from the king pin to a point on the vehicle centre line just in front of the rear axle.

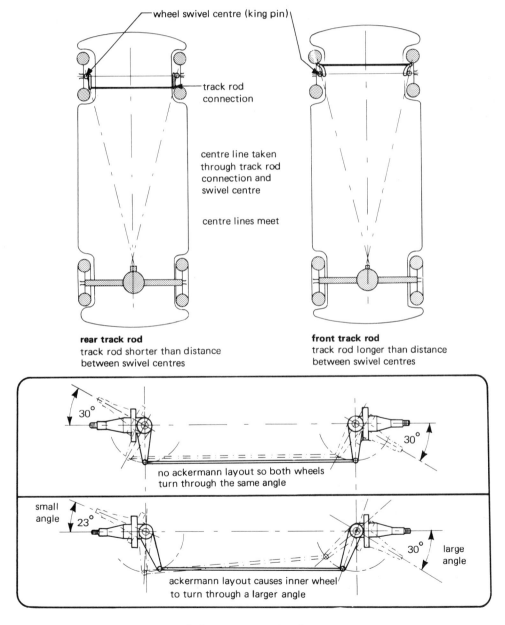

Ackermann steering layout

5.2 Braking Systems

Basic Features

Energy is required when a vehicle is accelerated from rest to a certain speed. A proportion of that energy is now stored in the vehicle and is called *kinetic energy*. In order to reduce the speed of the vehicle, the brakes have to convert the kinetic energy to *heat energy;* the speed of conversion governs the rate at which the vehicle slows down.

The work done by the moving vehicle to overcome the friction between a rotating disc and a stationary pad generates heat which is carried away by the air; the harder the pad is pushed against the disc, the greater will be the heat produced, but a limit is reached when the wheel skids.

Maximum braking is achieved when:

1 **all wheels are held on the verge of skidding,**
2 **adhesion between the tyre and road is excellent.**

Tyre adhesion depends on

1 type of road surface
2 condition of surface, e.g. wet, dry, greasy, state and design of tyre tread.

Types of Brake

There are two main types of brake:

1 drum,
2 disc.

Drum brakes

These have two shoes, anchored to a stationary back-plate, which are internally expanded to contact the drum by hydraulic cylinders or a mechanical linkage.

The end at which the shoe is anchored affects the retarding force it applies to the drum: the rotation of the drum gives a self-energizing action called *self-servo* which causes the

1 **leading shoe to be forced towards the drum,**
2 **trailing shoe to be forced away from the drum.**

The leading shoe is the first shoe after the expander in the direction of rotation.

Many cars have 2 L.S. front brakes and L. & T. rear brakes. The more powerful front brakes take advantage of the transference of weight from the rear to the front which occurs when the brakes are applied.

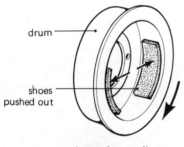

drum

shoes
pushed out

**internal expanding
drum brake**

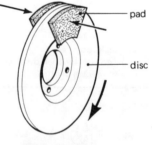

pad

disc

disc brake

Type	Advantages	Application
Leading and trailing shoes (L. & T.)	1 Easy to connect to hand brake linkage 2 Good braking action obtained when the vehicle is moving in reverse	Rear brakes
Two-leading shoes (2 L.S.)	1 Both shoes wear equally 2 More powerful brake; both shoes have a self-servo action 3 More stable action over a wide temperature range	Front brakes

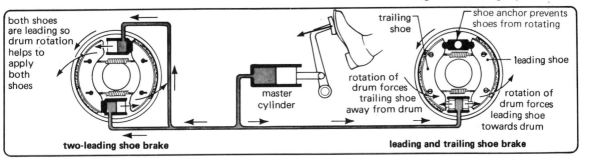

both shoes are leading so drum rotation helps to apply both shoes

trailing shoe

shoe anchor prevents shoes from rotating

leading shoe

rotation of drum forces trailing shoe away from drum

rotation of drum forces leading shoe towards drum

master cylinder

two-leading shoe brake

leading and trailing shoe brake

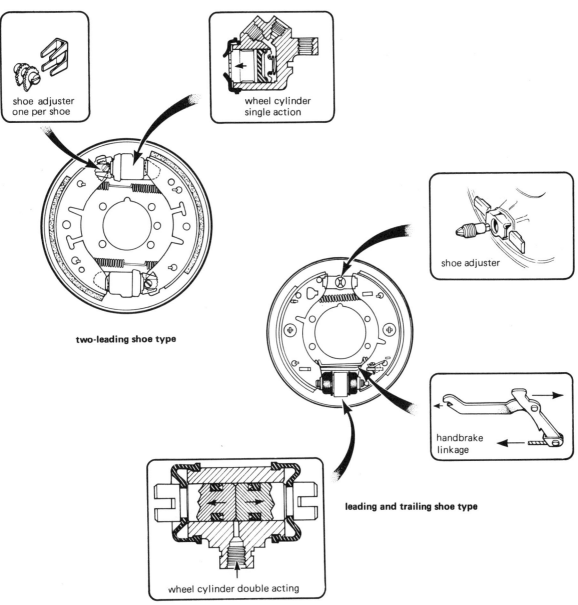

shoe adjuster one per shoe

wheel cylinder single action

two-leading shoe type

shoe adjuster

handbrake linkage

leading and trailing shoe type

wheel cylinder double acting

Types of drum brake

poor braking occurs when a drum brake gets very hot

heat from brake is more readily given up to the air

disc brakes can be used continuously for a longer period before brake fade occurs

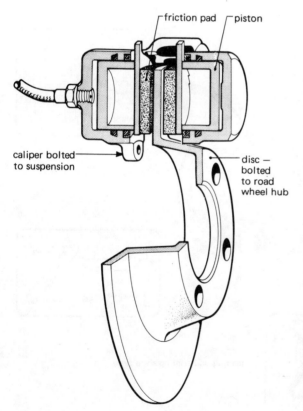

friction pad — piston

caliper bolted to suspension

disc — bolted to road wheel hub

Disc brakes

Exposed to the air, disc brakes radiate the heat to the air better than drum brakes: this means that the brake can be operated continuously for a longer period, i.e. they have a greater resistance to *fade* (fall-off in brake efficiency due to heat).

This fade resistance, and features such as automatic adjustment, make the disc brake a popular choice for the front wheels of a car. One drawback with many designs of disc brake is the absence of self-servo, so a vacuum servo is fitted to boost the effort applied by the driver.

Brake Operating Systems

The operating system can be
1 hydraulic
2 mechanical or
3 pneumatic (air)

Hydraulically operated systems

This system is used in most vehicles other than motor-cycles and heavy commercials. It has a high efficiency, is suited to vehicles that have independent suspension and is fully compensated in its operation. A fully compensated brake means that the driver's effort is shared between each brake, therefore no one brake can apply until all clearances at the other brakes have been taken up.

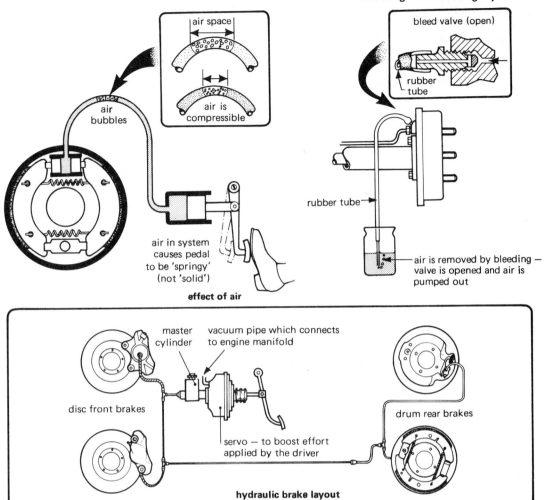

air space

air bubbles

air is compressible

air in system
causes pedal
to be 'springy'
(not 'solid')

effect of air

bleed valve (open)

rubber tube

rubber tube

air is removed by bleeding —
valve is opened and air is
pumped out

master cylinder

vacuum pipe which connects
to engine manifold

disc front brakes

drum rear brakes

servo — to boost effort
applied by the driver

hydraulic brake layout

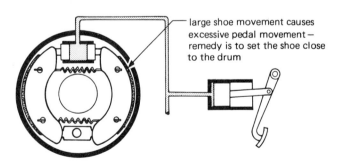

large shoe movement causes
excessive pedal movement —
remedy is to set the shoe close
to the drum

brake requiring adjustment

Hydraulic brake operation

Depression of the pedal pumps fluid through the pipes and moves the shoe (or pad) until it contacts the drum (disc). At this point the pedal feels 'solid' so from then onwards the force applied by the driver causes the fluid to become pressurized which in turn exerts a thrust on the brake cylinder piston and applies the brake. Release of the pedal allows the shoe return springs to pump the fluid back to the master cylinder.

Provision is made to allow air to be bled from the system after any part has been dismantled. Air, unlike brakefluid, is compressible, so if air is in any part of the system the pedal will be 'springy'.

The brakefluid used must flow freely, have a high boiling point and must not injure the rubber seals. *Only use the type recommended because complete failure can occur if the incorrect fluid is used.*

Legal requirements insist on mechanical operation of the brakes on at least two wheels. This is used in the event of failure of the hydraulic system and also for locking the wheels when the vehicle is parked.

Maintenance of Brake Systems

The following table should only act as a guide; the manufacturer's recommendations should always be followed.

Interval	Attention required	Note
Every 2000 km (About 1000 miles) or 1 month intervals	Check fluid level and top up if necessary	If frequent topping up is necessary, system should be examined for leaks
Every 10 000 km (About 5000 miles)	Check friction pads and linings. Adjust brakes which are adjustable types	Linings and pads should be free from oil and grease. Replace when thickness of: 1 pads approaches 2 mm 2 lining is less than one third of original thickness
Every 15 000 km (About 10 000 miles)	Check system for leaks and rubber hoses for weakness	Defective parts should be renewed
Every 40 000 km (About 24 000 miles) or 18 month intervals	Change fluid	Brake fluid absorbs water from the atmosphere: this lowers the boiling point of the fluid
Every 60 000 km (About 40 000 miles) or 3 year intervals	Renew operating components	All rubber parts should be replaced

5.3 Review Questions

1   On a beam axle the stub axle pivots about a
(a) king pin
(b) ball joint
(c) track rod
(d) track arm

2   Front wheel alignment is adjusted by altering the
(a) angle of the track arm
(b) length of the track rod
(c) distance between the king pins
(d) position of the drag link

3   The track rod is connected to the track arm by a
(a) ball joint
(b) king pin
(c) stub axle
(d) universal joint

4   Rotary motion of the steering wheel is converted to a reciprocating motion by the
(a) track arm
(b) track rod
(c) stub axle
(d) steering box

5   A collapsible steering column is one which collapses to
(a) damp out road vibrations
(b) improve safety for the driver
(c) simplify its removal for repair
(d) provide adjustment of the steering wheel

6   As applied to steering, the abbreviation P.A.S. stands for
(a) pump assisted system
(b) pump aided steering
(c) power activated system
(d) power assisted steering

7   When a vehicle is turning a corner, which road wheel is steered through the largest angle and which road wheel rotates the fastest?

	Largest angle	*Fastest*
(a)	Inside front	Outside front
(b)	Inside front	Outside rear
(c)	Outside front	Outside front
(d)	Outside front	Outside front

8   When a vehicle is cornering, each wheel should form a right angle to a line drawn from the
(a) centre line of the vehicle
(b) instantaneous centre of rotation
(c) centre of the rear axle
(d) mid-point of the front suspension system

9   A steering system has the track rod positioned in front of the stub axle centre line. The Ackermann layout is obtained by
(a) setting the track arms downwards and inwards
(b) having one track rod shorter than the other track rod
(c) making the track rod shorter than the distance between the swivel axis centres
(d) making the track rod longer than the distance between the swivel axis centres

10   A certain steering system has a track rod which is equal in length to the distance between the swivel axis centres. When the outer wheel is steered through 20° the angle steered by the inner wheel is
(a) less than 20°
(b) 20°
(c) more than 20° but less than 25°
(d) more than 25°

11   The purpose of a brake is to
(a) store energy
(b) change friction to heat
(c) convert energy to kinetic energy
(d) convert kinetic energy to heat energy

12   Which one of the following is necessary if a vehicle is to stop in the shortest distance possible?
(a) Brakes held on verge of skidding and excellent road adhesion
(b) Excellent road adhesion and all wheels set to skid
(c) All wheels set to skid and smooth, dry road surface
(d) Smooth, dry road surface and brakes held on verge of skidding

13   What is the effect on the leading shoe when it is applied to a brake drum which is rotating in a forward direction?
The shoe is pushed
(a) away from the drum
(b) towards the hydraulic expander
(c) away from the anchor pin
(d) harder into contact with the drum

14   Which shoe of a leading and trailing shoe brake does the most work and where is this shoe positioned?

	Most work	*Position*
(a)	Leading	First shoe after expander in d.o.r.
(b)	Leading	First shoe before expander in d.o.r.
(c)	Trailing	First shoe after expander in d.o.r.
(d)	Trailing	First shoe before expander in d.o.r.

15   As applied to a braking system, the term 'self-servo' means that the
(a) vehicle is fitted with a vacuum device
(b) trailing shoe is forced towards the drum
(c) pedal force increases as the brake gets hotter
(d) rotation of the drum helps to apply the brake

16   A vehicle has two wheels braked by a 2 L.S. system and two wheels braked by a L. & T. system. One reason for this layout is:
(a) the 2 L.S. front brakes are efficient when the vehicle is moving backwards
(b) the 2 L.S. rear brakes are easier to link-up with the hand brake
(c) the L. & T. front brakes have a self-servo action on all shoes
(d) the 2 L.S. front brakes take advantage of the weight transference

17   As applied to a braking system, the term 'brake fade' means the
(a) decrease in friction due to wear
(b) fall-off in efficiency due to heat
(c) increase in effort as the shoe clearance increases
(d) discolouration of the lining when it is oil-soaked

18   Compared with an internally expanded shoe brake, a disc brake has the advantage:
(a) greater resistance to fade
(b) fades at a lower temperature
(c) small effort gives large braking torque
(d) greater self-servo action at high speed

19   If the pedal of a hydraulically operated brake is 'springy' it indicates that the
(a) system contains air
(b) shoe clearance is excessive
(c) brake fluid should be changed
(d) system is in a good condition

20   The brake system should be dismantled if the reservoir was topped up with mineral oil instead of the correct brake fluid. This action is necessary because mineral oil
(a) is compressible
(b) will not pressurize
(c) damages the rubber seals
(d) boils at a lower temperature

6 Electrical System

6.1 Electrical Terms

In many ways electricity behaves like water, so
water is often used to help to understand the
common electrical terms.

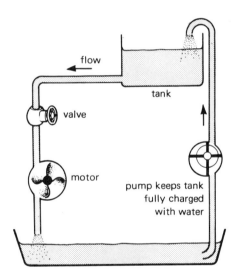 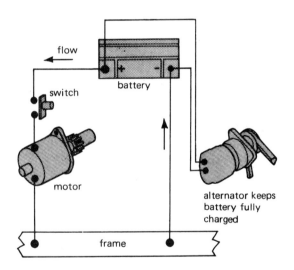

Subject	Water	Electricity
Carried by a:	pipe	cable
Pressure expressed in:	pascals (lbf/in²)	volts (V)
Flow measured in:	litres/s (gal/h)	ampere (A)
Flow caused by:	high level storage tank or pump	battery or dynamo or alternator
Flow controlled by the size of:	pipe	cable
Flow can only take place when:	tap is open	switch is closed and circuit is complete

Conductor

This applies to a material such as copper which freely allows a flow of electricity. A cable must be a good conductor.

Insulator

An insulator is a material which resists the flow of electricity. A cable is coated with an insulation material such as rubber or p.v.c. (plastics) to prevent the electrical energy taking another path to that which is intended.

Circuit

A circuit forms a continuous path for the electricity to flow from the source to the consuming device and back again to the source. An *open-circuit* is the term used when the circuit is incomplete; a *short-circuit* indicates .that a proportion of the electrical current is taking some other path due to poor insulation.

Fuse

A fuse is used to prevent damage and reduce the risk of fire as the result of a short circuit. A fuse melts when the flow of current is excessive.

6.2 Main Electrical Components

The complete electrical system consists of a number of separate sections or circuits. These are:

(a) Battery — supplies energy to operate the components which are needed when the engine is stationary or when the output from the charging system is low.

(b) Charging — supplies the electrical energy when the engine is running. Also maintains the battery in a fully charged state.

(c) Ignition — provides a spark to 'fire' the engine.

(d) Lighting — needed for exterior and interior illumination.

(e) Starting — enables the engine to be cranked over at a speed sufficient for it to 'fire'.

(f) Auxiliary — includes the various accessories such as windscreen wipers and washers, direction indicators etc.

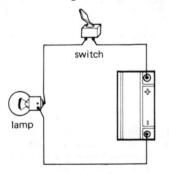
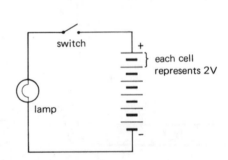

symbols may be used to represent electrical components

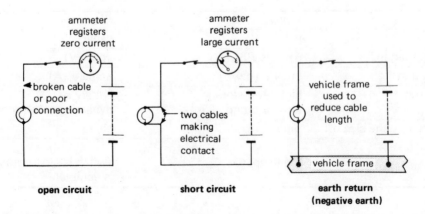

open circuit   **short circuit**   **earth return (negative earth)**

The Lead-acid Battery

The purpose of the battery is to store electrical energy. It does this by converting the electrical energy supplied to it into chemical energy so that when an electrical current is required the energy change is reversed.

Most vehicles use a lead-acid battery: this type has lead plates which are immersed in an electrolyte of sulphuric acid and distilled water.

Cell action

As the battery discharges (gives up its energy) the lead in the plates undergoes a chemical change and the acid becomes 'weaker', i.e. the relative density decreases.

To reverse the action an electrical charge is supplied from the alternator or dynamo. This changes the lead plates back to their original chemical forms and 'strengthens' the electrolyte. A charge current must pass through the battery in one direction only, so direct current (d.c.) is supplied with the positive ($+$) terminal of the charger connected to the positive terminal of the battery.

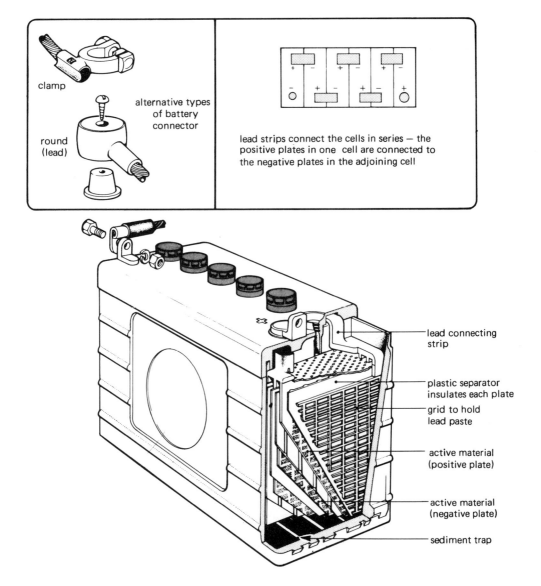

clamp

round
(lead)

alternative types
of battery
connector

lead strips connect the cells in series — the positive plates in one cell are connected to the negative plates in the adjoining cell

lead connecting strip

plastic separator insulates each plate

grid to hold lead paste

active material (positive plate)

active material (negative plate)

sediment trap

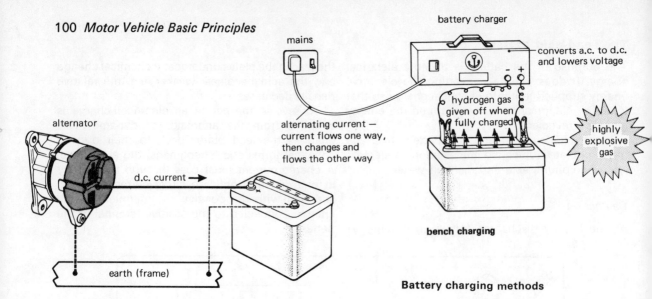

alternator

d.c. current →

earth (frame)

battery charging by the vehicle alternator

mains

alternating current —
current flows one way,
then changes and
flows the other way

battery charger

converts a.c. to d.c.
and lowers voltage

hydrogen gas
given off when
fully charged

highly
explosive
gas

bench charging

Battery charging methods

Battery Tests

Hydrometer

The relative density (also called specific gravity) of the electrolyte is measured by a hydrometer, and from the readings the state of charge can be determined. Typical values are:

fully charged	1·280
half charged	1·200
fully discharged	1·150

High rate discharge tester

This indicates the ability of a battery to supply a large current similar to that required to operate the starter motor. The tester shows the battery voltage during the time that a large current is being 'drawn' from the battery.

This is a severe test and must not be prolonged more than necessary. It should only be applied to a fully charged battery.

Care and Maintenance

Battery fitting

Extensive damage to electrical components having diodes and transistors will result if the earth polarity of the vehicle is reversed by fitting the battery the incorrect way.

Mounting bolts and brackets should hold the battery firm, but the bolts should not be over-tightened.

Electrolyte level

This level should be maintained at the correct level, e.g. 6 mm above the plates, by topping up with *clean distilled water*. Frequent topping up indicates overcharging.

Terminal corrosion

Corrosion is reduced by coating the terminals with vaseline. A corroded terminal is cleaned by immersing the terminal in ammoniated warm water or soda dissolved in water.

Acid preparation

It is sometimes necessary when concentrated sulphuric acid has to be diluted to 1·280 for filling a new battery. A glass or earthenware container should be used and for safety purposes:

the acid is added slowly to the water.

An acid burn should be treated immediately with sodium bicarbonate solution or, failing this, clean water.

Acid splashes on clothes should be neutralized with an alkali, such as ammonia, if holes are to be avoided.

Charging Systems

The generator converts mechanical energy to electrical energy.

There are two types of generator:

1 dynamo,
2 alternator.

Both types generate alternating current but they differ in the way in which they rectify or change the current from alternating to the direct current needed for battery charging.

Alternators are commonly used today because they have a higher efficiency than a dynamo. Extra care must be taken by the mechanic to avoid damage to the semi-conductor devices used to rectify and regulate the output of an alternator. A surge in voltage such as occurs when a cable is accidentally flashed is one way in which the unit is damaged, so for component safety the battery terminal should be removed when working on, or around, the alternator.

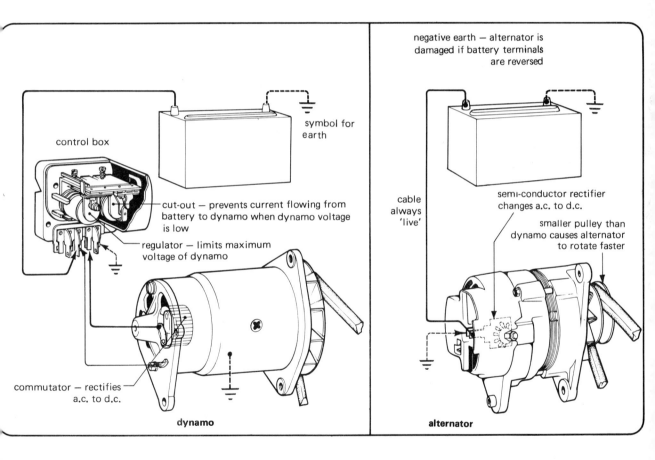

Charging systems

The Lighting System

The law specifies the number, position, type and minimum rating of lamps.

A simple circuit consists of a battery, switch and lamp bulb. Closing the switch causes the bulb filament to glow which provides illumination.

A lighting circuit consists of a number of lamp bulbs all connected in *parallel* and controlled by three switches:

switch 1 operates the side and rear lamps. It also supplies:

switch 2 which operates the headlamps and supplies:

switch 3 which distributes the current to either the main-beam or dip-beam lamps.

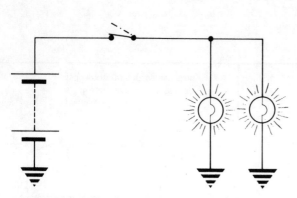

lamps in parallel
full battery voltage applied in both lamps — both lamps will operate at full brilliance

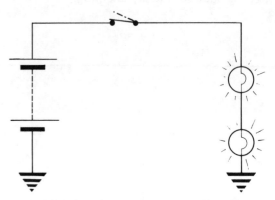

lamps in series
reduced voltage applied to lamps — poor illumination: failure of one lamp 'switches off' the other lamp

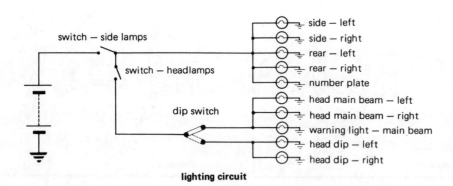

lighting circuit

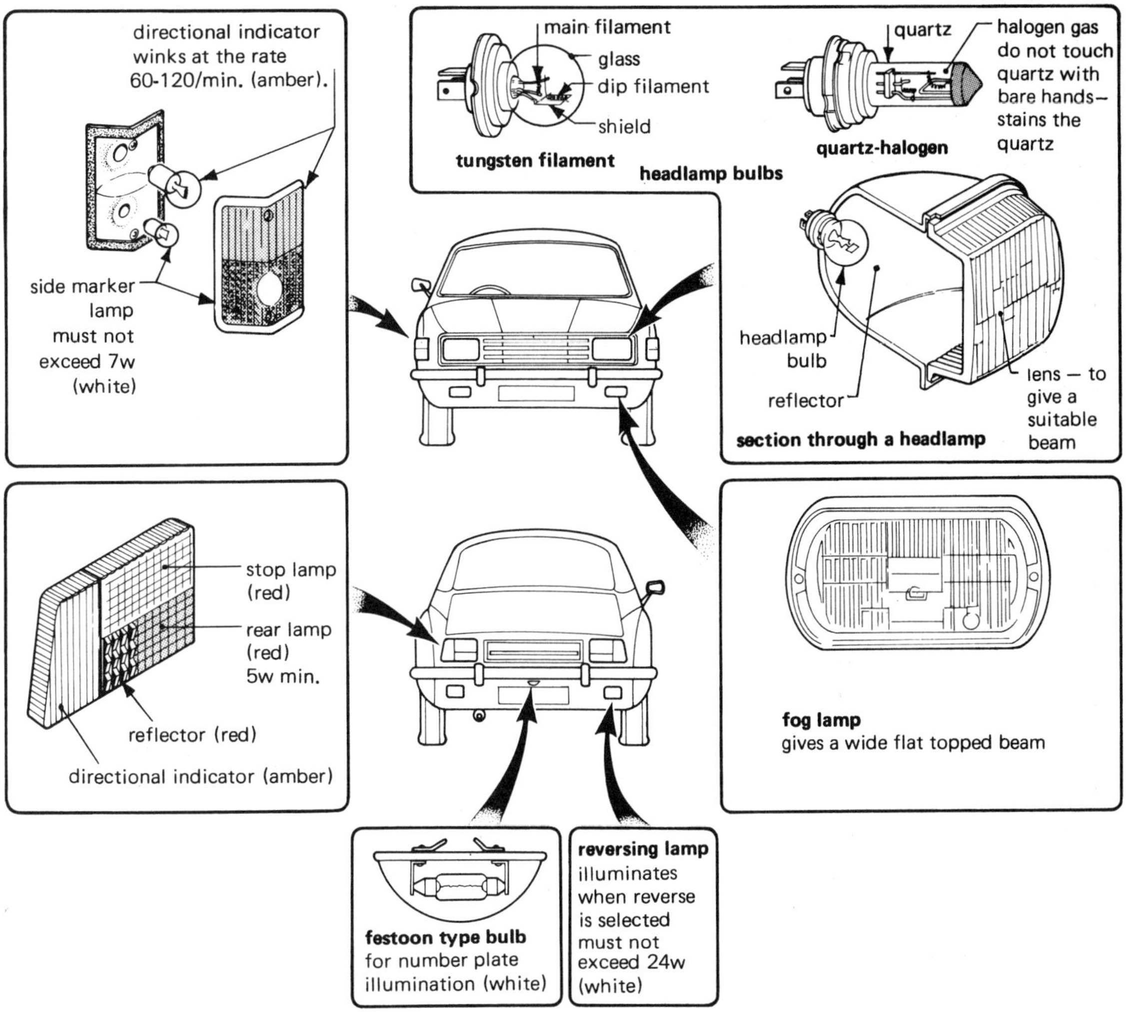

directional indicator winks at the rate 60-120/min. (amber).

side marker lamp must not exceed 7w (white)

main filament
glass
dip filament
shield

tungsten filament

headlamp bulbs

quartz

halogen gas do not touch quartz with bare hands— stains the quartz

quartz-halogen

headlamp bulb

reflector

lens — to give a suitable beam

section through a headlamp

stop lamp (red)

rear lamp (red) 5w min.

reflector (red)

directional indicator (amber)

fog lamp
gives a wide flat topped beam

festoon type bulb
for number plate illumination (white)

reversing lamp
illuminates when reverse is selected must not exceed 24w (white)

Lamp positions

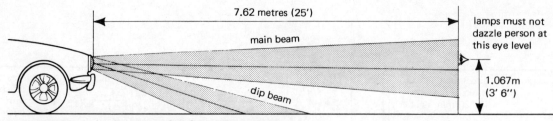

7.62 metres (25')

main beam

lamps must not dazzle person at this eye level

dip beam

1.067m (3' 6")

to avoid dazzle the headlamp beam is deflected downwards

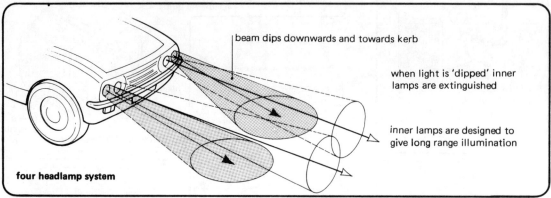

beam dips downwards and towards kerb

when light is 'dipped' inner lamps are extinguished

inner lamps are designed to give long range illumination

four headlamp system

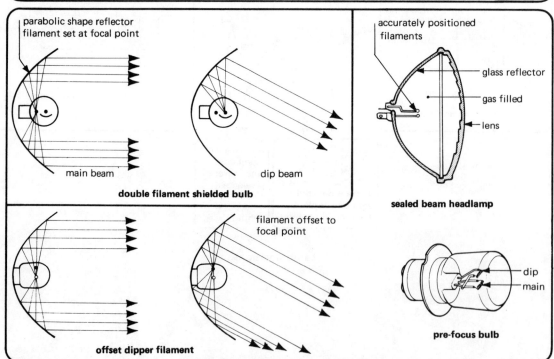

parabolic shape reflector filament set at focal point

main beam

dip beam

double filament shielded bulb

accurately positioned filaments

glass reflector

gas filled

lens

sealed beam headlamp

filament offset to focal point

offset dipper filament

dip

main

pre-focus bulb

Anti-dazzle arrangements

Cables and Terminals

Most electrical cables are made of copper and stranded to give flexibility: insulation is obtained by coating the wire with p.v.c.

Cable sizes are given as the number of strands and the diameter of each strand: e.g. 44/0·30 means 44 strands of wire of diameter 0·30 mm

Defective cables should be replaced by a cable of similar size. The size of a cable for a new circuit can be based on the recommendation that each strand of diameter 0·30 mm can carry 0·5 ampere.

For identification purpose cables are colour coded.

Terminals

Those used for general circuits are generally of the 'quick connect' type.

Starter Circuit

On a cold morning the battery may have to supply a current in excess of 200 A to rotate the engine. For this reason thick cables of short length are needed to connect the battery to the starter motor.

The modern pre-engaged starter motor uses a solenoid to mesh the pinion initially with the engine flywheel ring gear. When the gear is fully engaged the motor is operated and the engine is turned.

Pinion engagement on older type cars was obtained by an *inertia* type drive: the reluctance of the pinion to revolve when the starter was operated caused it to move along helical splines and engage suddenly with the flywheel.

Cable size	Safe current (ampere)	Uses
61/0·90	300	Starter lead
44/0·30	27	Main feeds to circuits
28/0·30	17	Headlamps
14/0·30	8	Lightly loaded circuits

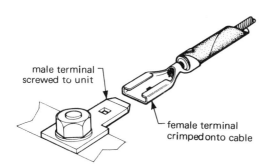

quick connect type

male terminal screwed to unit

female terminal crimped onto cable

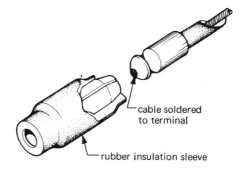

bullet type

cable soldered to terminal

rubber insulation sleeve

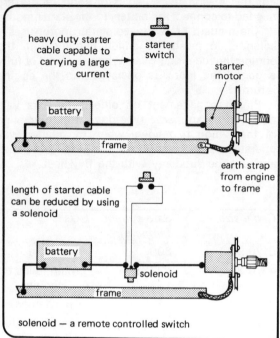

heavy duty starter cable capable to carrying a large current

starter switch

starter motor

battery

frame

earth strap from engine to frame

length of starter cable can be reduced by using a solenoid

battery

solenoid

frame

solenoid — a remote controlled switch

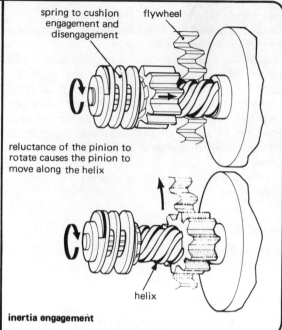

spring to cushion engagement and disengagement

flywheel

reluctance of the pinion to rotate causes the pinion to move along the helix

helix

inertia engagement

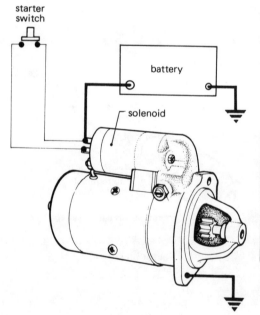

starter switch

battery

solenoid

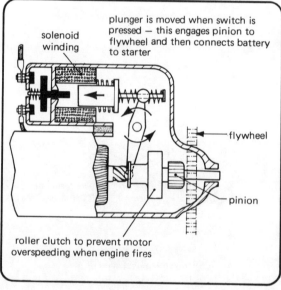

plunger is moved when switch is pressed — this engages pinion to flywheel and then connects battery to starter

solenoid winding

flywheel

pinion

roller clutch to prevent motor overspeeding when engine fires

pre-engage starter motor

Starter motor

6.3 Review Questions

1 A fuse in an electrical circuit 'blows' as the result of a high
(a) voltage caused by a short circuit
(b) current flow caused by a short circuit
(c) voltage caused by an open circuit
(d) current flow caused by an open circuit

2 The electrolyte used in a lead-acid battery is
(a) sulphuric acid and diluted lead
(b) diluted lead and pure water
(c) pure water and distilled water
(d) distilled water and sulphuric acid

3 What type of electrical current is needed to charge a battery and what is the effect of this current on the electrolyte density?

	Type of current	Effect on density
(a)	A.C.	Increases
(b)	A.C.	Decreases
(c)	D.C.	Increases
(d)	D.C.	Decreases

4 The relative density of the electrolyte in a lead-acid battery is 1·280. This value indicates that the battery is
(a) fully discharged
(b) half charged
(c) three-quarters charged
(d) fully charged

5 The ability of a battery to supply a current similar to that required by the starter motor is tested by
(a) a wide scaled hydrometer
(b) a high rate discharge tester
(c) a voltmeter scaled 0–200 V
(d) an ammeter scaled 0–100 A

6 The need to top up a battery at frequent intervals indicates that the
(a) battery is being overcharged
(b) charging rate is too low
(c) electrical system is shorting to earth
(d) battery stoppers are not sealing the cell

7 A 12V lead–acid battery consists of
(a) three cells in series
(b) six cells in series
(c) three cells in parallel
(d) six cells in parallel

8 A spark must not be produced when a fully charged battery is either being disconnected from a bench charger or being fitted to a vehicle because the
(a) gas leaving the cells is highly explosive
(b) gas produced by a sudden battery discharge is corrosive
(c) spark and gas reacts to form dangerous fumes
(d) spark can cause the battery polarity to reverse

9 The electrolyte level in a lead–acid battery should be checked periodically: if the level is low the battery should be topped up with
(a) diluted acid
(b) clean distilled water
(c) sulphuric acid having a relative density of 1·280
(d) an electrolyte similar to that used in the battery

10 One reason why an alternator produces a higher output than a dynamo is because the alternator
(a) is driven faster
(b) has a commutator
(c) generates direct current
(d) always uses a 'negative earth'.

11 If the battery polarity is reversed on a vehicle fitted with an alternator, the effect will be:
(a) the fan belt will slip
(b) the cut-out will not operate
(c) the lights will be dimmer than normal
(d) the semi-conductor devices will be damaged

12 A lighting circuit includes two headlamps. What is the effect on the illumination if the filament in the right-hand headlamp is broken?

	Left-hand lamp	Right-hand lamp
(a)	No light	No light
(b)	Dim	Brighter than normal
(c)	Normal	No light
(d)	Dim	Dim

13   An earth return lighting circuit includes two headlamps. What is the effect on the illumination if the earth connection on the right-hand headlamp is causing an open circuit?

	Left-hand lamp	Right-hand lamp
(a)	No light	No light
(b)	Dim	Brighter than normal
(c)	Normal	No light
(d)	Dim	Dim

14   An electrical cable is classified as 28/0·30. This means that the cable

(a) has 28 strands, each strand of diameter 0·30 mm

(b) has a diameter of 28 mm, each strand of diameter 0·30 mm

(c) consists of 28 strands, each strand will carry 0·3 A safely

(d) will carry 28 A, each strand taking 0·3 A

15   A thick cable is needed to supply the starter motor because

(a) the motor requires a very large current

(b) the voltage needed is higher than 200 V

(c) thick insulation is needed to prevent a short circuit

(d) extra strength is needed to resist the vibration

7 Appendix

7.1 Answers to Review Questions

Section 1.3   Page 18

1. b	2. a	3. d	4. c	5. b
6. a	7. a	8. c	9. a	10. d
11. d	12. b	13. d	14. c	15. d
16. a	17. b	18. a	19. c	20. a

Section 2.7   Page 50

1. d	2. d	3. a	4. b	5. c
6. d	7. d	8. c	9. b	10. c
11. b	12. b	13. c	14. a	15. c
16. a	17. b	18. a	19. c	20. c
21. a	22. b	23. c	24. d	25. c
26. c	27. a	28. d	29. b	30. a
31. a	32. b	33. a	34. c	35. a
36. b	37. b	38. c	39. a	40. d
41. a	42. d	43. a	44. a	45. b
46. c	47. a	48. c	49. d	50. b
51. c	52. a	53. d	54. a	55. b
56. d	57. a	58. d	59. c	60. c
61. b	62. b	63. b	64. d	65. d
66. a	67. a	68. d	69. a	70. a

Section 3.5   Page 70

1. b	2. d	3. a	4. b	5. c
6. b	7. c	8. c	9. a	10. d
11. c	12. d	13 c	14 b	15. a
16. d	17. d	18. d	19. b	20. d
21. b	22. c	23. a	24. c	25. c
26. b	27. d	28. b	29. b	30. d

Section 4.5   Page 85

1. a	2. d	3. c	4. b	5. a
6. a	7. d	8. a	9. d	10. b
11. a	12. d	13. c	14. d	15. c
16. c	17. a	18. c	19. b	20. c

Section 5.3   Page 95

1. a	2. b	3. a	4. d	5. b
6. d	7. a	8. b	9. d	10. b
11. d	12. a	13. d	14. a	15. d
16. d	17. b	18. a	19. a	20. c

Section 6.3   Page 107

1. b	2. d	3. c	4. d	5. b
6. a	7. b	8. a	9. b	10. a
11. d	12. c	13. c	14. a	15. a

7.2 English-American Glossary

English	American
alternator	a.c. generator
axle beam	solid axle
body wing	fender
bush (metal or rubber)	bushing
car bonnet	hood
car boot	trunk
contact-breaker	breaker
drop arm	Pitman arm
dynamo	generator
earth, electrical	ground
foot brake	service brake
gearbox	transmission
gear lever	gear shift lever
gudgeon pin	piston pin
inlet manifold	intake manifold
integral body	unibody
petrol	gasoline
relief valve	regulator valve
silencer	muffler
spanner	wrench
sump	oil pan
swept volume (cylinder)	piston displacement
tappet	valve lifter
track	wheel tread
track arm	steering arm
track rod	tie rod
transmission system	drive line or system
windscreen	windshield

Index

absorber, shock 13
acid, battery 100
Ackermann layout 89
advance, spark 23
    automatic 38
air springs 75
alternating current 100
alternator 97, 100
ampere 97
anti-freeze 47
arch, wheel 84
arcing at contacts 38
arm, rocker 25
    steering 87
    track 87
articulated vehicle 16
atomization, fuel 32, 42
axle, beam 13
    rear 12
    shaft 68
    stub 87
banjo axle casing 68
battery 14, 97–102
    lead acid 99
b.d.c. 21
bearing, big-end 23
    main 23
    shell 23
bellows thermostat 47
bevel gears 65
big-end 23
bleeding, brake 93
blower 41
bore 21
box, steering 87
brake 9, 14, 90–4
    disc 14, 90–4
    drum 14, 90–4
    hand 91
    shooting 16
bulb, lamp 103
cables 105
cam 24
camshaft 25
    drive 26
    overhead 24, 26

capacitor 38
capacity, engine 21
car, private 14
carburettor 22, 31–5
    constant-vacuum 34
    types 34
cell, battery 98
chamber, combustion 24,
                    25, 42
    float 32
    mixing 32
channel frame section 10
chemically correct
                mixture 31
choke 32–4
    constant 34
    tube 31
    variable 34
circuit, low tension 38
    open and closed 98
    primary 38
    secondary 38
cleaner, air 36
clearance, valve 24, 25
clutch 12, 55
    dog 58, 61
    faults 57
    fluid 55
    friction 55
    single plate 57
coil, ignition 38
combustion, internal 10
compensating system 34
compression stroke 21, 40
condenser 38
conduction 44
conductor, electrical 98
constant velocity joint 64
contact breaker 38
convection 44
convertible 16
cooling, air 44
    engine 44
    liquid 44
correction system 34
corrosion 82, 100

cotters, valve 24
coupe 16
crankshaft 20
crashing of gears 60
cross-ply tyres 78
cross type universal
                joint 63
crown wheel 65
current, alternating 100
    direct 100
cut-out 101
cycle, motor 18, 44
cylinder 20
    four 27
    master; clutch 56
    multi 26
    six 28
    wheel 91

damper 13, 73, 75
deflector piston 30
density, relative 47, 100
depression 31
dermatitis 43
derv, 11, 40
diaphragm type clutch 56
diesel 10, 11, 16, 40
differential 12, 65
direct current 100
disc brake 14
discharge tester 100
distortion, frame 10
distributor, ignition 38
double de-clutching 61
doughnut type universal
                joint 63
draught, up and down 32
drive arrangements 14
drophead car 16
drum brake 14
dynamo 101
earth, electrical 98
    negative 98
electrolyte 99
energy, heat 14, 90
    kinetic 14, 90

engine 9, 10, 20
    compression-ignition 10,
                    11, 40
    heat 10
    horizontally opposed 29
    spark-ignition 10, 29
    vee 28
estate car 16
exhaust stroke 21
expansion, gas 20

fade, brake 92
fan 45
fifth wheel 18
filament, lamp 103
filter 48
filtration, fuel 42
final drive 12, 65
floating, semi and fully 68
flywheel 23
four-stroke, compression
                ignition 41
    spark-ignition 21, 22
frame 9, 10, 82
    sections 82
fuel systems 37, 42
    pumps 37
fuse 98

gallery, main oil 48
gas, exhaust 31
gasoline 11
gearbox 12, 57
    automatic 55, 59
    constant mesh 59, 61
    manual 59
    shafts 57
    sliding mesh 57
    synchro mesh 59, 61
gearing, bevel 65
    hypoid 65
    types of 57
generator 14
geometry, steering 88
governor, C.1. 41
gravity, specific 100

gross train weight (g.t.w.) 18
gross vehicle weight (g.v.w.) 16
guide, valve 24
halogen 103
handbrake 91
Hardy Spicer universal joint 63
heavy commercial vehicles 16, 40, 65
helical gearing 57, 61
helical road spring 74
high tension lead 39
hooke type universal joint 63
horizontally opposed engines 29
Hotchkiss drive 74
hub construction 69, 87
hydrogen 100
hydrometer, battery 100
  cooling system 47
hypoid final drive 65
ignition, coil 38
  compression 10, 40
  magneto 38
  pre 44
  spark 10, 21, 29
  system 38
  transistorized 38
indicator, direction 103
induction stroke 21, 40
inertia engagement 105
injection, fuel 42
injector 42
instantaneous centre of rotation 88
insulator 98
integral frame 10, 82
interval, firing 27, 28, 29
jacket, water 45
jet 31
  progression 33
  slow-running 33
joints, sliding 62
  steering 87
  universal 62
kinetic energy 14
knock, diesel 42
laminated or leaf spring 73
lamps 103, 104
layrub type universal joint 63
layshaft, gearbox 57
lead-acid battery 99
leading and trailing brake shoes 90
leading shoe 90
leading shoe, two 90
legal regulations, brakes 94
  tyres 81

lighting 102–04
link, drag 87
lozenging, frame 10
lubrication, boundary 48
  engine 48
  full film 48
  gearbox 61
  splash 49
mainshaft 57
manifold, exhaust 36
  induction 35
member, cross 10
  side 10
mixture, rich and weak 31
oil 48
open type drive 74
operation, cycles of 21, 22, 40
order, firing 27
Otto cycle 21
oversteer 81
parabolic reflector 104
petrol 11, 31
pick up 16
pin, crank 23
  king 87
pinion, final drive 65
pipe, induction 32
piston 20
  rings 21
plug, sparking 38
pneumatic suspension 75
ports, transfer 30, 31
  two stroke 29
power stroke 21
pre-ignition 44
pressurized cooling system 47
primary shaft, gearbox 57
pump, distributor 43
  fuel feed; C.I. 42
  injection 42
  in-line 43
  jerk 43
  oil 48
  petrol 37
  water 46
quartz 103
radial-ply tyres 78
radiation 44
radiator 45
ratio, air/fuel 31
  compression 21, 40
  petrol-oil; two-stroke 29
reach, sparking plug 38

reflector, lamp 103
  parabolic 104
regulator 101
retard spark 23
rigid vehicle 16, 17
rim, wheel 79
rings, oil control 49
  piston 21
rod, connecting 20, 23
  push 25
  track 87
rotor 39
rubber springs 75
S.A.E. number 48
saloon car 16
scuttle, body 84
sealed beam lamp 104
self-servo 90
semi-conductors 101
servo 93
shackle, spring 74
shaft, axle 68
  drive 62
  gearbox 57
  half 68
  propeller 62
shell, body 9, 10, 82
shock absorber 13
silencer, air 36
sill, body 84
single-plate clutch 57
slow running system 33
small end 22
solenoid 106
sparking plug 38
spiral bevel gear 65
splash lubrication 49
spring, road 73
  valve 20
spur gearing 57
starter motor 106
starting, cold 33, 34
steering 9, 131, 87–9
  power assisted 88
strangler 32
stroke 20
  four 21
  power 21
  two 29, 41
sump, wet; lubrication 48
suspension 9, 13
  independent 13, 77
tappet 24
t.d.c. 21, 23
teeth, dog 58
telescopic damper 76
terminals 105

thermostat 46
thermo-syphon cooling 44
throttle 32–34
timing, ignition 23, 38
  port 30
  valve 24
torque reaction 74
torsion bar springing 75
track arm 87
  rod 87
tractor 18
trailer 18
trailing shoe, brake 91
transmission 9, 10, 55
tube, choke 31
tunnel, propeller shaft 65, 84
two-stroke compression ignition 41
  spark ignition 29
tyres, adhesion of 90
  types 78
universal joint 62
  constant velocity 64
unsprung weight 77
valance, wing; body 84
valve, bleed 93
  clearance 24
  exhaust 20
  inlet 20
  operation 24
  overhead 25
  relief 48
  side 25
  spring 21
  timing 24, 26
  tyre 81
van 16
vaporization, fuel 32
venturi 31
viscosity, oil 48
volt 97
volume, swept and clearance 21
wagon, station 16
wax type thermostat 46
well based wheel rim 79
wheelbase 17
wheel, fifth 18
  types 78
whip, propeller shaft 72
wing, body 84